D0286419

Key Element Guide
ITIL® Service Strategy

London: TSO

information & publishing solutions

Published by TSO (The Stationery Office) and available from:

Online
www.tsoshop.co.uk

Mail, Telephone, Fax & E-mail
TSO
PO Box 29, Norwich, NR3 1GN
Telephone orders/General enquiries:
0870 600 5522
Fax orders: 0870 600 5533
E-mail: customer.services@tso.co.uk
Textphone 0870 240 3701

TSO@Blackwell and other Accredited Agents

The AXELOS swirl is a trade mark of AXELOS Limited

ITIL® is a registered trade mark of AXELOS Limited

P3O® is a registered trade mark of AXELOS Limited

MSP® is a registered trade mark of AXELOS Limited

PRINCE2® is a registered trade mark of AXELOS Limited

The AXELOS logo is a trade mark of AXELOS Limited

The Best Management Practice Official Publisher logo is a trade mark of AXELOS Limited

First edition Crown copyright 2008
Second edition Crown copyright 2012

Third impression 2014

ISBN 9780113313600 (Single copy ISBN)
ISBN 9780113313655 (Sold in a pack of 10 copies)

Printed in the United Kingdom for The Stationery Office

Material is FSC certified and produced using ECF pulp, sourced from fully sustainable forests.

P002500763   c18   07/12

Contents

Acknowledgements

AUTHOR

David Cannon, BMC Software

KEY ELEMENT GUIDE AUTHORING TEAM

Ashley Hanna, HP

Lou Hunnebeck, Third Sky Inc.

Vernon Lloyd, Fox IT

Stuart Rance, HP

Randy Steinberg, Migration Technologies Inc.

REVIEWERS

Best Management Practice and The Stationery Office would like to thank itSMF International for managing the quality assurance of this publication, and the following reviewers for their contributions:

Duncan Anderson, Global Knowledge; John Donoghue, Allied Irish Bank plc; John Earle, itSMF Ireland Ltd; Robert Falkowitz, Concentric Circle Consulting; Padraig Farrell, SureSkills; Siobhan Flaherty, Generali PanEurope; Signe Marie Hernes Bjerke, Det Norske Veritas; Michael Imhoff Nielsen, IBM; Jackie Manning, Bord Gáis Networks; Krikor Maroukian, King's College London; Reiko Morita, Ability InterBusiness Solutions Inc.; Trevor Murray, The Grey Matters; Gary O'Dwyer, Allied Irish Banks plc; Benjamin Orazem, SRC d.o.o.; Sue Shaw, TriCentrica; Marco Smith, iCore Ltd; Hon P Suen, ECT Service Ltd; and Paul Wigzel, Paul Wigzel Training and Consultancy.

1 Introduction

This key element guide is intended to provide a summary of the basic concepts and practice elements of *ITIL Service Strategy*, which forms part of the core ITIL publication suite.

ITIL is a set of best-practice publications for IT service management (ITSM).[1] ITIL provides guidance on the provision of quality IT services, and on the capabilities needed to support them. ITIL is not a standard that has to be followed; it is guidance that should be read and understood, and used to create value for the service provider and its customers. Organizations are encouraged to adopt ITIL best practices and to adapt them to work in their specific environments in ways that meet their needs.

ITIL is the most widely recognized framework for ITSM in the world. In the 20 years since it was created, ITIL has evolved and changed its breadth and depth as technologies and business practices have developed.

The section numbering in this key element guide is not the same as the section numbers in the core publication, *ITIL Service Strategy*. Therefore, do not try to use references to section numbers in the core publication when referencing material in this key element guide.

1.1 THE ITIL SERVICE LIFECYCLE

The ITIL framework is based on five stages of the service lifecycle as shown in Figure 1.1, with a core publication providing best-practice guidance for each stage. This guidance includes

---

[1] ITSM and other concepts from this chapter are described in more detail in Chapter 2.

Figure 1.1 The ITIL service lifecycle

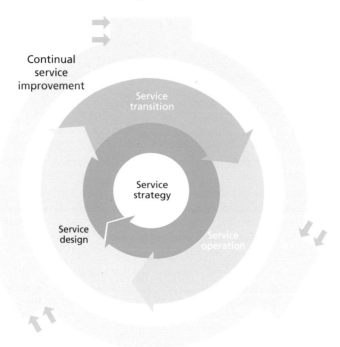

principles, processes and activities, organization and roles, technology, challenges, critical success factors, and risks. The service lifecycle uses a hub-and-spoke design, with service strategy at the hub, and service design, service transition and service operation as the revolving lifecycle stages or 'spokes'. Continual service improvement surrounds and supports all stages of the service lifecycle. Each stage of the lifecycle exerts influence on the others and relies on them for inputs and feedback. In this way, a constant set of checks and balances ensures that as business demand changes, the services can adapt and respond effectively.

In addition to the core publications, there is also a complementary set of ITIL publications providing guidance specific to industry sectors, organization types, operating models and technology architectures.

The following key characteristics of ITIL contribute to its global success:

- **Vendor-neutral** ITIL service management practices are not based on any particular technology platform or industry type. ITIL is owned by the UK government and is not tied to any commercial proprietary practice or solution.
- **Non-prescriptive** ITIL offers robust, mature and time-tested practices that have applicability to all types of service organization. It continues to be useful and relevant in public and private sectors, internal and external service providers, small, medium and large enterprises, and within any technical environment.
- **Best practice** ITIL represents the learning experiences and thought leadership of the world's best-in-class service providers.

1.2   SERVICE STRATEGY – KEY ELEMENT GUIDE

ITIL Service Strategy provides best-practice guidance for the service strategy stage of the service lifecycle.

1.2.1   Purpose and objectives of service strategy

The purpose of the service strategy stage is to define the perspective, position, plans and patterns that a service provider needs to be able to execute to meet an organization's business outcomes.

The objectives of service strategy include providing:

- An understanding of what strategy is
- A clear identification of the services and an understanding of the customers who use them
- The ability to define how value is created and delivered
- A means to identify opportunities to provide services and how to exploit them
- A service provision model that articulates how services will be delivered and funded, to whom they will be delivered and for what purpose
- The means to understand the organizational capability required to deliver the strategy
- Documentation and coordination covering how service assets are used to deliver services, and how to optimize their performance
- Processes that define the strategy of the organization, which services will achieve the strategy, what level of investment will be required, at what levels of demand, and the means to ensure that a working relationship exists between the customer and service provider.

1.2.2   Scope

ITIL Service Strategy starts by defining and discussing the generic principles and processes of service management, and then goes on to describe how they are applied consistently to the management of IT services.

Service strategy is intended for use by both internal and external service providers, and includes guidance for organizations which offer IT services as a profitable business, as well as those which offer IT services to other business units within the same organization.

Two aspects of strategy are covered in *ITIL Service Strategy*:

- Defining a strategy whereby a service provider will deliver services to meet a customer's business outcomes
- Defining a strategy for how to manage those services.

1.2.3   Value to business

Adopting and implementing standard and consistent approaches for service strategy will:

- Support the ability to link activities performed by the service provider to outcomes that are critical to customers
- Give the service provider a clear understanding of what services will make its customers successful, and enable it to organize itself optimally to deliver and support those services
- Enable the service provider to respond quickly and effectively to changes in the business environment
- Support the creation and maintenance of a portfolio of quantified services that will enable the business to achieve positive return on its investment in services
- Facilitate communication between the customer and the service provider.

1.3   CONTEXT

Each core ITIL publication addresses those capabilities that have a direct impact on a service provider's performance. The core is expected to provide structure, stability and strength to service management capabilities, with durable principles, methods and tools. This serves to protect investments and provide the necessary basis for measurement, learning and improvement.

1.3.1   Service strategy

At the centre of the service lifecycle is service strategy. Value creation begins here with understanding organizational objectives and customer needs. Every organizational asset, including people, processes and products, should support the strategy.

ITIL Service Strategy provides guidance on how to view service management not only as an organizational capability but as a strategic asset. It describes the principles underpinning the practice of service management which are useful for developing service management policies, guidelines and processes across the service lifecycle.

Organizations already practising ITIL can use *ITIL Service Strategy* to guide a strategic review of their service management capabilities and to improve the alignment between those capabilities and their business strategies. *ITIL Service Strategy* will encourage readers to stop and think about *why* something is to be done before thinking of *how*.

1.3.2   Service design

Service design is the stage in the lifecycle that turns a service strategy into a plan for delivering business objectives. *ITIL Service Design* provides guidance for the design and development of services and service management practices. It covers design principles and methods for converting strategic objectives into portfolios of services and service assets. The scope of *ITIL Service Design* includes the changes and improvements necessary to increase or maintain value to customers over the lifecycle of services, the continuity of services, the achievement of service levels, and conformance to standards and regulations.

1.3.3   Service transition

ITIL Service Transition provides guidance for the development and improvement of capabilities for introducing new and changed services into supported environments. It describes how to transition an organization from one state to another while controlling risk and supporting organizational knowledge for decision support. It ensures that the value(s) identified in the service strategy, and encoded in the service design, are effectively transitioned so that they can be realized in service operation.

1.3.4   Service operation

ITIL Service Operation describes best practice for managing services in supported environments. It includes guidance on achieving effectiveness and efficiency in the delivery and support of services to ensure value for the customer, the users and the service provider. *ITIL Service Operation* provides guidance on how to maintain stability in service operation, even while allowing for changes in design, scale, scope and service levels.

1.3.5   Continual service improvement

ITIL Continual Service Improvement provides guidance on creating and maintaining value for customers through better strategy, design, transition and operation of services. It combines principles, practices and methods from quality management, change management and capability improvement.

ITIL Continual Service Improvement describes best practice for achieving incremental and large-scale improvements in service quality, operational efficiency and business continuity, and for ensuring that the service portfolio continues to be aligned to business needs.

2 Service management as a practice

2.1 SERVICES AND SERVICE MANAGEMENT

2.1.1 Services

Definitions

Service: A means of delivering value to customers by facilitating outcomes customers want to achieve without the ownership of specific costs and risks.

IT service: A service provided by an IT service provider. An IT service is made up of a combination of information technology, people and processes. A customer-facing IT service directly supports the business processes of one or more customers and its service level targets should be defined in a service level agreement. Other IT services, called supporting services, are not directly used by the business but are required by the service provider to deliver customer-facing services.

Outcome: The result of carrying out an activity, following a process, or delivering an IT service etc. The term is used to refer to intended results, as well as to actual results.

An outcome-based definition of service moves IT organizations beyond business–IT alignment towards business–IT integration. Customers seek outcomes but do not wish to have accountability or ownership of all the associated costs and risks. The customer can judge the value of a service based on a comparison of cost or price and reliability with the desired outcome. Customer satisfaction is also important. Customer expectations keep shifting, and a service provider that does not track this will soon lose business.

2.1.2 Service management

Business would like IT services to behave like other utilities such as water, electricity or the telephone. Simply having the best technology does not ensure that the IT service will provide utility-like reliability. Service management can bring this utility quality of service to the business.

> **Definitions**
>
> *Service management:* A set of specialized organizational capabilities for providing value to customers in the form of services.
>
> *Service provider:* An organization supplying services to one or more internal or external customers.

The more mature a service provider's capabilities are, the greater is their ability to meet the needs of the customer. The act of transforming capabilities and resources into valuable services is at the core of service management. The origins of service management are in traditional service businesses such as airlines, banks and hotels.

2.1.3 IT service management

Every IT organization should act as a service provider, using service management to ensure that they deliver outcomes required by their customers. A service level agreement (SLA) is used to document agreements between an IT service provider and a customer. An SLA describes the service, documents targets, and specifies the responsibilities of the service provider and the customer.

2.1.4   Service providers

There are three main types of service provider:

- **Type I – internal service provider** This type is embedded within a business unit. There may be several Type I service providers within an organization.
- **Type II – shared services unit** An internal service provider that provides shared IT services to more than one business unit.
- **Type III – external service provider** A service provider that provides IT services to external customers.

IT service management (ITSM) concepts are often described in the context of only one of these types. In reality most organizations have a combination of IT service provider types.

2.1.5   Stakeholders in service management

Stakeholders have an interest in an organization, project or service etc. and may also be interested in the activities, targets, resources or deliverables. There are many stakeholders inside the service provider. There are also many external stakeholders, for example:

- **Customers** Those who buy goods or services. Customers define and agree the service level targets.
- **Users** Those who use the service on a day-to-day basis.
- **Suppliers** Third parties responsible for supplying goods or services that are required to deliver IT services.

There is a difference between internal customers and external customers:

- **Internal customers** These work for the same business as the service provider – for example, the marketing department uses IT services.
- **External customers** These work for a different business from the service provider. External customers typically purchase services by means of a legally binding contract or agreement.

2.1.6   Utility and warranty

From the customer's perspective, value consists of achieving business objectives. The value of a service is created by combining utility (fitness for purpose) and warranty (fitness for use).

- **Utility** is the ability to meet a particular need. It is often described as 'what the service does' – for example, a service that enables a business unit to process orders.

- **Warranty** is an assurance that the service will meet its agreed requirements. Warranty includes the ability of a service to be available when needed, to provide the required capacity, and to provide the required reliability in terms of continuity and security.

The value of a service is only created when both utility and warranty are designed and delivered.

Information about the desired business outcomes, opportunities, customers, utility and warranty of the service is used to develop the definition of a service. Using an outcome-based definition helps to ensure that managers plan and execute all aspects of service management from the customer's perspective.

2.1.7   Best practices in the public domain

Organizations benchmark themselves against peers and seek to close gaps in capabilities. This enables them to become more competitive. One way to close gaps is the adoption of best practices. There are several sources for best practice including public frameworks, standards and the proprietary knowledge of organizations and individuals. ITIL is the most widely recognized and trusted source of best-practice guidance for ITSM.

2.2   BASIC CONCEPTS

2.2.1   Assets, resources and capabilities

The relationship between service providers and customers revolves around the use of assets – both those of the service provider and those of the customer. The performance of customer assets is a primary concern for service management.

Definitions

Asset: Any resource or capability.

Customer asset: Any resource or capability used by a customer to achieve a business outcome.

Service asset: Any resource or capability used by a service provider to deliver services to a customer.

There are two types of asset – resources and capabilities. Resources are direct inputs for production. Capabilities represent an organization's ability to coordinate, control and deploy resources to produce value. It is relatively easy to acquire resources compared to capabilities. Figure 2.1 shows examples of capabilities and resources.

Figure 2.1 Examples of capabilities and resources

Capabilities	Resources
Management	Financial capital
Organization	Infrastructure
Processes	Applications
Knowledge	Information
People (experience, skills and relationships)	People (number of employees)

2.2.2 Processes

Definition: process

A process is a structured set of activities designed to accomplish a specific objective. A process takes one or more defined inputs and turns them into defined outputs.

Process characteristics include:

- **Measurability** We can measure the process in a relevant manner.
- **Specific results** The process delivers specific results, which must be individually identifiable and countable.

- **Customers** The process delivers its primary results to a customer or stakeholder. Customers may be internal or external to the organization.

- **Responsiveness to specific triggers** The process should be traceable to a specific trigger.

The outputs from the process should be driven by the process objectives. Process measurement and metrics can be built into the process to control and improve the process as illustrated in Figure 2.2.

Figure 2.2 Process model

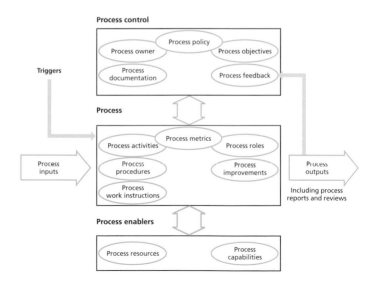

2.2.3 Organizing for service management

Best practices described in ITIL need to be tailored to suit organizations and situations. The starting point for organizational design is service strategy.

2.2.3.1 Functions

A function is a team or group of people and the tools or other resources they use to carry out one or more processes or activities. In larger organizations, a function may be performed by several departments, teams and groups. In smaller organizations, one person or group can perform multiple functions – for example, a technical management department could also incorporate the service desk function.

ITIL Service Operation describes the following functions:

- **Service desk** The single point of contact for users. A typical service desk manages incidents and service requests, and also handles communication with the users.
- **Technical management** Provides technical skills and resources needed to manage the IT infrastructure throughout the service lifecycle.
- **IT operations management** Executes the daily operational activities needed to manage IT services and the supporting IT infrastructure.
- **Application management** Is responsible for managing applications throughout their lifecycle. This differs from application development which is mainly concerned with one-time activities for requirements, design and build of applications.

The other core ITIL publications rely on the technical and application management functions described in *ITIL Service Operation*, but they do not define any additional functions in detail.

2.2.3.2   Roles

The core ITIL publications provide guidelines and examples of role descriptions. In many cases roles will need to be combined or separated.

> **Definition: role**
>
> A role is a set of responsibilities, activities and authorities granted to a person or team. A role is defined in a process or function. One person or team may have multiple roles – for example, the roles of configuration manager and change manager may be carried out by a single person.

Roles are often confused with job titles but they are not the same. Each organization defines job titles and job descriptions, and individuals holding these job titles can perform one or more roles. See Chapter 5 for more details about roles and responsibilities.

2.2.4   The service portfolio

The service portfolio is the complete set of services managed by a service provider, and it represents the service provider's commitments and investments across all customers and market spaces. It consists of three parts:

- **Service pipeline** Services that are under consideration or development, but are not yet available to customers. The service pipeline is a service provider's business view of possible future services.

- **Service catalogue** Live IT services, including those available for deployment. It is the only part of the service portfolio that is published to customers. It includes a customer-facing view (or views) of the IT services. It also includes information about supporting services required by the service provider.

■ **Retired services** Services that have retired.

Service providers often find it useful to distinguish customer-facing services from supporting services:

■ **Customer-facing services** are visible to the customer. These normally support the customer's business processes and facilitate outcomes desired by the customer.
■ **Supporting services** support or 'underpin' the customer-facing services. These are typically invisible to the customer, but are essential to the delivery of customer-facing services.

Figure 2.3 illustrates the components of the service portfolio. These are important components of the service knowledge management system (SKMS) described in section 2.2.5.

Figure 2.3 The service portfolio and its contents

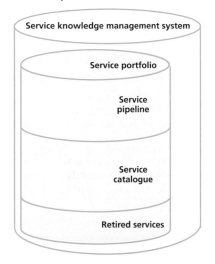

2.2.5   Knowledge management and the SKMS

Knowledge and information enable people to perform activities and support information flow between lifecycle stages and processes. Implementing knowledge management enables effective decision support and reduces risks.

ITIL Service Transition describes an architecture for a service knowledge management system (SKMS) with four layers:

- **Presentation layer** Enables searching, browsing, retrieving, updating, subscribing and collaboration. Different views are provided for different audiences.
- **Knowledge-processing layer** Where information is converted into knowledge which enables decision-making.
- **Information integration layer** Provides integrated information from data in multiple sources in the data layer.
- **Data layer** Includes tools for data discovery and collection, and data items in unstructured and structured forms.

2.3   GOVERNANCE AND MANAGEMENT SYSTEMS

2.3.1   Governance

Governance defines the common directions, policies and rules that both the business and IT use to conduct business.

> **Definition: governance**
>
> Ensures that policies and strategy are actually implemented, and that required processes are correctly followed. Governance includes defining roles and responsibilities, measuring and reporting, and taking actions to resolve any issues identified.

Governance applies a consistently managed approach at all levels of the organization by ensuring a clear strategy is set, and by defining the policies needed to achieve the strategy.

2.3.2 Management systems

Many businesses have adopted management system standards for competitive advantage, to ensure a consistent approach in implementing service management, and to support governance.

An organization can adopt multiple management system standards, such as:

- A quality management system (ISO 9001)
- An environmental management system (ISO 14000)
- A service management system (ISO/IEC 20000)
- An information security management system (ISO/IEC 27001)
- A management system for software asset management (ISO/IEC 19770).

As there are common elements between such management systems, they should be managed in an integrated way rather than having separate management systems.

ISO management system standards use the Plan-Do-Check-Act (PDCA) cycle shown in Figure 2.4. This PDCA cycle is used in each of the core ITIL publications.

Definition: ISO/IEC 20000

An international standard for IT service management.

ISO/IEC 20000 is an international standard that allows organizations to prove best practice in ITSM. Part 1 specifies requirements for the service provider to plan, establish, implement, operate, monitor, review, maintain and improve a

Figure 2.4 Plan-Do-Check-Act cycle

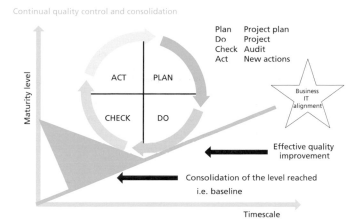

service management system (SMS). One of the most common routes for an organization to achieve the requirements of ISO/IEC 20000 is by adopting ITIL.

2.4   THE SERVICE LIFECYCLE

The service lifecycle is an organizing framework, supported by the organizational structure, service portfolio and service models within an organization. See Chapter 1 for an introduction to each ITIL service lifecycle stage.

2.4.1   Specialization and coordination across the lifecycle

Organizations should function in the same manner as a high-performing sports team. Each player in a team and each member of the team's organization who are not players position themselves to support the goal of the team. Each player and team member has a different specialization that contributes to the whole. The team matures over time taking into account feedback from experience, best practice and current processes and procedures to become an agile high-performing team.

Specialization allows for expert focus on components of the service but components of the service also need to work together for value. Coordination across the lifecycle creates an environment focused on business and customer outcomes instead of just IT objectives and projects. Specialization combined with coordination helps to manage expertise, improve focus and reduce overlaps and gaps in processes.

Adopting technology to automate the processes and provide management information that supports the processes is also important for effective and efficient service management.

2.4.2   Processes through the service lifecycle

Each core ITIL publication includes guidance on service management processes as shown in Table 2.1.

Most ITIL roles, processes and functions have activities that take place across multiple stages of the service lifecycle. For example:

■ Service validation and testing may design tests during the service design stage and perform these tests during service transition

■ Technical management provides input to strategic decisions about technology, and assists in the design and transition of infrastructure

Table 2.1 The processes described in each core ITIL publication

Core ITIL lifecycle publication	Processes described in the publication
ITIL Service Strategy	Strategy management for IT services
	Service portfolio management
	Financial management for IT services
	Demand management
	Business relationship management
ITIL Service Design	Design coordination
	Service catalogue management
	Service level management
	Availability management
	Capacity management
	IT service continuity management
	Information security management
	Supplier management

Table continues

Table 2.1 *continued*

Core ITIL lifecycle publication	Processes described in the publication
ITIL Service Transition	Transition planning and support
	Change management
	Service asset and configuration management
	Release and deployment management
	Service validation and testing
	Change evaluation
	Knowledge management
ITIL Service Operation	Event management
	Incident management
	Request fulfilment
	Problem management
	Access management
ITIL Continual Service Improvement	Seven-step improvement process

■ Business relationship managers assist in gathering requirements during the service design stage of the lifecycle, and take part in the management of major incidents during the service operation stage.

The strength of the service lifecycle relies on continual feedback throughout each stage of the lifecycle. At every point in the service lifecycle, monitoring, assessment and feedback drives decisions about the need for minor course corrections or major service improvement initiatives.

3   Service strategy principles

3.1   STRATEGY

A strategy is a plan (or set of plans) that outlines how an organization will meet a designed set of objectives.

A service strategy defines how a service provider will use services to achieve the business outcomes of its customers, thereby enabling the service provider to meet its objectives.

An IT strategy focuses on how an organization intends to use and organize technology to meet its business objectives. An IT strategy typically includes an IT service strategy.

3.1.1   Fundamental aspects of strategy

Strategic thinking is based on the following fundamental aspects:

- Strategy uses theory to determine a solution to a business problem or objective.
- Strategy is focused on the value of the service provider to customers.
- Strategic decisions are determined by whether the service provider can continue to enable customers to meet their business outcomes – not simply by whether the service provider can meet its own objectives.
- Processes and tools that manage services effectively and efficiently are the basis for competitive advantage, and should be seen as strategic assets.
- Conflict and opposing objectives are characteristic of every organization. Strategy identifies the trade-offs involved, and enables the organization to decide how to deal with them.
- Strategy is a means to outperform competitors.

- Strategy is needed by commercial entities, government and non-profit organizations, but for different reasons and it might be defined and executed differently.

3.1.2   The four Ps of strategy

There are four forms of strategy that should be present, as illustrated in Figure 3.1.

The four Ps are:

- **Perspective** Vision and direction. A strategic perspective articulates what the business of the organization is, how it interacts with the customer and how its services or products will be provided.
- **Positions** How the service provider will compete against other service providers. Positions refer to the attributes and capabilities that set the service provider apart from competitors.
- **Plans** How the service provider will transition from its current situation to achieve its perspective and positions.
- **Patterns** Ongoing, repeatable actions that a service provider must perform to meet its strategic objectives.

Figure 3.1 Perspective, positions, plans and patterns

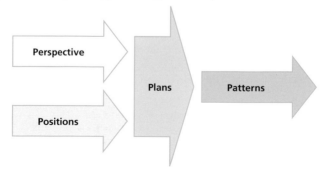

The four Ps are used throughout service strategy, but especially in the process of strategy management for IT services (see section 4.1).

3.1.2.1   The relationship between the four Ps

The four Ps are sometimes used to describe how an organization moves from perspective and positions, through planning, resulting in neatly conforming patterns. However, an organization is continuously changing, and perspectives, positions and plans are adapted accordingly.

3.2   CUSTOMERS AND SERVICES

3.2.1   Customers

Definitions

Customer: Someone who buys goods or services. The customer of an IT service provider is the person or group who defines and agrees the service level targets.

User: A person who uses the IT service on a day-to-day basis. Users are distinct from customers, as some customers do not use the IT service directly.

3.2.1.1   Internal and external customers

Service strategies vary depending on whether customers are internal or external. The main differences are listed in Table 3.1.

Table 3.1 Differences between internal and external customers

	Internal customers	External customers
Funding	Funding for IT services is provided internally – IT is a cost that needs to be recovered.	External customers fund the service directly. IT becomes a generator of income for the organization. The cost of the service, plus a margin, is recovered from the customer.
Link to business strategy and objectives	The service provider has the same organizational objectives and strategy as its customers. Ideally, the service provider and customer work together to deliver external services and optimize operational efficiency and effectiveness.	The objectives and strategies of the service provider and the customer are different. The customer's objectives are set by its executives and are appropriate for its business. The service provider's objective is to sustain its business by providing IT services.

Table continues

Table 3.1 *continued*

	Internal customers	External customers
Accounting	The cost of service is the primary driver. The aim is to provide an optimal balance between the cost and quality of the service – to support the organization in achieving its objectives.	The cost of the service is normally not disclosed to the customer. The price of the service is the primary driver.
Involvement in service design	Customers tend to be involved in detailed design specifications, often covering both functionality and manageability of the service – since both of these impact the level of investment required.	Customers may get involved in design work during needs-based and demand-based positioning. Typically, customers are not involved in design work and the service provider does not calculate the customer's return on investment.

Table continues

Table 3.1 *continued*

	Internal customers	External customers
Involvement in service transition and operation	Customers are often involved in building, testing and deploying services. Changes have to be assessed and approved by customers and IT managers. Customers are involved in defining deployment procedures, mechanisms and schedules.	Customer involvement in change management is clearly documented in the contract, along with clauses about how changes will impact service pricing. Requests for change are assessed by the customer in terms of impact and price. Customers are generally not involved in detailed design and testing of services, and have little visibility into the processes that manage these. Involvement in deployment is usually carefully scripted, and customers are trained in how to execute deployment activities.

Table continues

Table 3.1 *continued*

	Internal customers	External customers
Drivers for improvement	Improvements are driven by impact on the business, optimizing the balance between cost and quality and helping business units meet their objectives. Improvements are also aimed at improving the way services are designed, delivered and managed. Customers are often involved in the detail of service improvement plans, as they have skills which could help IT become better service providers.	Improvements are driven by the need to retain customers that contribute to the profitability of the service provider, and to remain competitive in the market. Changes that impact pricing and profitability drive measures that reduce cost while providing competitive service levels. Customers are not often involved in defining and executing service improvement plans, instead focusing on the expected results.

3.2.1.2 Business units as customers
Theoretically, IT and other business units focus on the same objectives, but in reality they often have different or opposing objectives. Sometimes this is deliberate corporate strategy – at other times it is just poor implementation of corporate strategy.

In either event, the IT department can find itself between conflicting demands of the 'corporation' as a whole and individual business units.

Service strategy should identify how to deal with these situations, and obtain the support of executives. In some cases this will mean accommodating conflicting requirements (which will need additional funding); in others IT will have to impose corporate objectives onto business units.

3.2.1.3   Other IT organizations as customers

Some IT organizations encourage their staff to view every IT unit as a customer, to promote higher-quality work and positive interactions between departments. While the objective is commendable, in reality all IT units are service providers to the business, and it is important to avoid any negative behaviour resulting from a contrived customer–supplier relationship.

3.2.1.4   IT as an external service provider

Although most examples in *ITIL Service Strategy* refer to internal service providers, the publication also covers the provision of IT services to external customers. Service providers are therefore described as either 'internal' or 'external'.

3.2.2   Services

Definition: service

A means of delivering value to customers by facilitating outcomes that customers want to achieve without the ownership of specific costs and risks.

ITIL uses service provision (rather than manufacturing) as a model, so the output of IT is seen as a set of services rather than products. IT delivers services which contribute value for customers. It does not focus on the output but on what the customer is able to do with the output.

Products and services are different in many ways, as shown in Table 3.2.

Table 3.2 Differences between services and manufactured products

Services	Manufactured products
Dynamic interactions between a service provider and customer.	Physical entities produced by processing raw materials or assembling components.
Delivered in real time as customers need and use them.	Created ahead of time and stored before distribution to customers.
Produced and consumed at the same time; services cannot be separated from their providers.	Produced by one entity; can be stored, distributed and sold by different entities at different times.
The output of a service is volatile, often changing in real time depending on the customer's environment.	The output of production is predictable; products should not deviate from a predefined norm by more than specific levels.

Table continues

Table 3.2 *continued*

Services	Manufactured products
The way in which services are delivered can vary with every iteration of service delivery.	Although variable production methods are used, each type of product generally follows exactly the same route through the factory.
A service's success can only be determined if the customer achieves a desired outcome.	A product's success is determined by the quality and delivery of the product itself.
The value of a service is only realized when it is actually used by a customer.	Value is created and realized every time a product changes hands.
The value of a service is carried in the relationship between the customer and service provider.	The value of a product is carried in the product itself.
Quality of a service is usually defined by the level of customer satisfaction based on subjective experience.	Quality is first based on whether the product meets predefined physical criteria, and only subsequently on the customer's experience.

3.2.2.1 Outcomes

An outcome is the result of carrying out an activity, following a process, delivering an IT service, etc. In *ITIL Service Strategy*, outcomes are referred to as 'business outcomes' or 'customer outcomes' and are defined as follows:

■ **Business outcomes** Used in the context of internal customers, where the outcome represents the overall business objectives of both the business unit and the internal service provider

■ **Customer outcomes** Used in the context of external service providers, where the service provider's outcomes are based on the customer's outcomes, but are different.

The definition of a service specifically refers to *outcomes* and not *outputs*. An output is delivered by the service provider; the outcome refers to whether the customer could use the output to achieve their desired objectives. What is delivered is less important than whether the customer could achieve what they envisaged when using the service.

3.2.2.2   Responsibility for specific costs and risks

Customers are concerned about what a service will cost and how reliable it will be. Good customer relationships do not, however, depend on the customer knowing about every expenditure item and risk mitigation measure.

The customer is primarily interested in the outcome, and does not need to be concerned with specific costs and risks that the service provider will incur. The customer will only be exposed to the total price of the service, and can judge the value by comparing price and reliability with the desired outcome. However, in order to reassure a customer of the level of performance or safety of a product or service, the service provider might provide more detailed information.

It is the service provider's responsibility to work out the most efficient and effective way of providing the service and the best way to communicate the cost. If the customer wants to pay less, they should be prepared to reduce their requirements for functionality or performance, or else forgo the service altogether.

3.2.2.3   Internal and external services

Just as there are internal and external customers, there are internal and external services (see Figure 3.2). Internal services are delivered between departments or business units in the same organization. External services are delivered to external customers.

It is important to differentiate between services that support an internal activity and those that actually achieve business outcomes. Although the difference may not appear significant since the activity to deliver the services is similar, internal services must be linked to external services before their contribution to business outcomes can be understood and measured.

IT services

An IT service is a service provided to one or more customers by an IT service provider. The service is based on the use of information technology and supports the customer's business processes. It is made up of a combination of people, processes and technology.

There are three types of IT service, as shown in Table 3.3.

Figure 3.2 Internal and external services

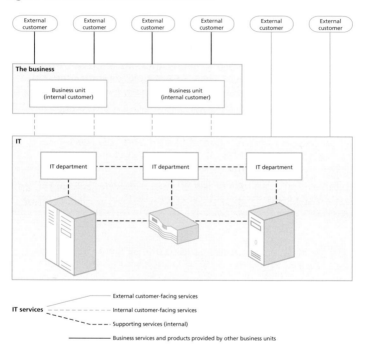

Table 3.3 Types of IT service

Type of service	Definition
Supporting service	A service that is not directly used by the business, but is required by the IT service provider so that it can provide other IT services – for example, directory services, or communication services.
Internal customer-facing service	An IT service that directly supports a business process managed by another business unit – for example, sales reporting service, enterprise resource management.
External customer-facing service	An IT service that is directly provided to an external customer – for example, internet access at an airport.

Business services and products provided by other business units

Definition: business service

A service that is delivered to business customers by business units – for example, delivery of financial services to customers of a bank, or goods to the customers of a retail store. Successful delivery of business services often depends on one or more IT services.

Although an internal service provider is not directly responsible for the business's services and products, it is responsible for providing IT services which will enable outcomes to be met. Thus it is important that IT knows what the business's services are, how the business uses IT services and how these services are measured. This will have a direct impact on IT's contribution to the organization.

3.2.2.4 Core, enabling and enhancing services

All services, whether internal or external, can be further classified as:

- **Core services** Deliver basic outcomes desired by one or more customers. They represent the value that the customer wants and for which they are willing to pay.
- **Enabling services** Essential for a core service to be delivered. Enabling services may or may not be visible to the customer. The customer does not perceive them as services in their own right.
- **Enhancing services** Added to a core service to make it more exciting. They are non-essential for the delivery of a core service, but encourage customers to use the core service more (or to choose a particular core service in preference to others provided by competitors).

3.2.3 Value

The value of a service can be defined as the level to which that service meets a customer's expectations. It is often measured by how much the customer is willing to pay for the service.

Unlike products, services do not have much intrinsic value. The value of a service comes from what it enables someone to do. Its value is not determined by the provider, but by the person who receives it – because they decide what they will do with the service and what return they will achieve. Services contribute value to an organization only when their value is perceived to be higher than the cost of obtaining the service.

The characteristics of value are:

- Value is defined by the customer.
- Customers must perceive that the service has the best mix of features for the price they are willing to pay.
- The service must support the ability of customers to meet their objectives.
- Value changes over time – a service provider should track a customer's changing needs and adjust its service accordingly.

Value can only be calculated if three pieces of information are known:

- What service(s) did IT provide?
- What did the service(s) achieve in business terms?
- How much did the service(s) cost, or what was the price of the service(s)?

3.2.3.1   Creating value

Value is defined not only in terms of the customer's business outcomes; it also depends on the customer's perceptions and preferences. Perceptions are influenced by attributes of a service, present or prior experiences, and relative capability of competitors and peers. Perceptions are also influenced by the customer's self-image or position in the market, such as being an innovator, market leader or risk taker. The preferences and perceptions of customers affect how they assess the value of a particular offering or service provider over another.

Understanding and communicating value requires the service provider to develop a marketing mindset. Marketing in this context involves not only advertising services to influence customer perception, but also understanding the customer's context and requirements, and ensuring that services provide outcomes that are important to the customer.

3.2.3.2 Value added and value realized

Figure 3.3 shows a value chain where a number of IT components are used to deliver a service.

Figure 3.3 Money spent, value added and value realized

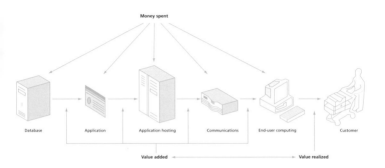

In Figure 3.3, each component is managed by a department in IT. Money is spent on procuring, developing and maintaining each component, and each department spends money on salaries, office space, benefits etc. As each department manages its component and makes sure that it is working effectively, it adds value to the service. For example, a database on its own has relatively little value, but an application combined with a database has a value that is higher than just the cost of the two components. When combined with application hosting, the service becomes even more valuable.

The secret to adding value is that every time another step is added to the service, the value of the service must grow at a higher rate than the amount of money spent. In other words, after each step in the value chain the service provider should be able to ask, 'If we sold what we have now, would it be of greater value than what we have spent on it?'

In a commercial model the service provider can only confirm that value was added if the customer paid more for the service than it actually cost. In the public sector the external customer is usually the tax payer. There are some rules to adding value:

- The amount of value added can only be calculated once value has been realized (once the service has achieved the desired outcome). In Figure 3.3 this happens when the customer achieves the desired outcome.
- The value realized must be greater than the money spent. This is true whether measured in financial terms (for example, how much money the customer paid for the service) or in non-financial terms (for example, could the local government process the planned number of driver's licence applications per day?)
- If the value realized is not greater than the money spent, then the service provider has not added any value. Rather, they have simply spent money (and made a loss).

These rules also apply to IT departments. Specifically:

- If IT wants to show that it has added value, it must link its activities to where the business realizes value.
- If IT is unable to do this, it will be perceived as a money-spending organization, not a value-adding organization.
- The only way a money-spending organization can demonstrate value is by cutting costs. This results in a vicious circle: IT is not perceived as adding value, so the business demands that it cuts costs, but then its ability to add value is reduced even more and the business demands more cost-cutting.

So how does IT ensure that it is perceived as a value adder, rather than a money spender? The secret lies in linking IT activities to services, and then linking those services to outcomes. In other words, IT should not be undertaking activities unless it can show that each activity helps to achieve the business outcome.

3.2.3.3 Linking 'value added' to 'value realized'

Services provided by an internal service provider will only be perceived as adding value if they can be linked to a service for an external customer. If there is no linkage to an external service, they will be viewed as 'money spent'. Supporting services are at least one more step removed from the external services. This does not mean that the service provider should disclose all internal services to the customer. Rather, the service provider should measure the contribution of each internal service to business outcomes.

The value of a service may be enhanced even further by providing it alongside other services. The concept of service packages is defined in section 3.4.8 of this publication.

3.2.3.4 Value capture

Value capture is the ability of a service provider to retain some of the value that has been created and realized. The ability of a service provider to differentiate itself and offer more value over time depends on obtaining funding to develop and improve services. Value capture is a good way of obtaining this funding since it links the cost of development to the service.

Value capture is an important notion for all types of service provider, internal and external. Good business sense discourages stakeholders from making major investment in any organizational capability unless it demonstrates value capture. Internal providers are encouraged to adopt this strategic perspective to continue as viable concerns within a business. Profits or surpluses allow continued investments in service assets that have a direct impact on capabilities.

3.2.4   Utility and warranty

Utility is the functionality offered by a product or service to meet a particular need. Utility can be summarized as 'what the service does'. Utility refers to those aspects of a service that contribute to tasks associated with achieving outcomes. Utility is also defined as any attribute of a service that removes, or reduces the effect of, constraints on the performance of a task.

Warranty is a guarantee that a product or service will meet its agreed requirements. Warranty refers to the ability of a service to be available when needed, to supply the required capacity and to provide specified reliability in terms of continuity and security. This is often described as being 'fit for use' or 'how the service is delivered'. Warranty is any attribute of a service that increases the potential of the business to be able to perform a task.

Utility is what the service does, and warranty is how it is delivered. Customers cannot benefit from something that is fit for purpose but not fit for use, and vice versa. The value of a service is therefore only delivered when both utility and warranty are designed and delivered.

3.2.4.1   The effects of improved utility and warranty on a service

Improving the utility of a service increases the functionality, or what it does for the customer, thus increasing the type and range of outcomes that can be achieved. Warranty does not automatically stay the same when utility is increased; maintaining consistent warranty when increasing utility requires good planning and increased investment. This investment is required for making changes to processes and tools, training, hiring additional employees to do the extra work, additional tools to perform newly automated activities etc.

Improving warranty of a service means that the service will continue to do the same things, but more reliably. Therefore there is a higher probability that the desired outcomes will be achieved, along with a decreased risk that the customer will suffer losses due to variations in service performance. Improved warranty also results in an increase in the number of times a task can be performed within an acceptable level of cost, time and activity. The improvement in service asset performance results in the ability to achieve business outcomes more consistently.

The warranty effect means that the performance of the **service assets** is improved. The utility effect means that the performance of the **customer assets** is improved.

Figure 3.4 shows how the concepts of utility and warranty influence strategic IT decisions; services are placed in the quadrant according to their warranty and utility levels, as well as their value to the customer. The chart shows services that have higher utility but lower warranty. These services have a utility bias.

Figure 3.4 also shows services that have lower utility than warranty (services that are reliable, but their functionality does not meet customer requirements fully). These services have a warranty bias. Services that have the appropriate levels of both warranty and utility are balanced – such services have functionality that consistently meets customer requirements.

Figure 3.4 Combined effects of utility and warranty on customer assets

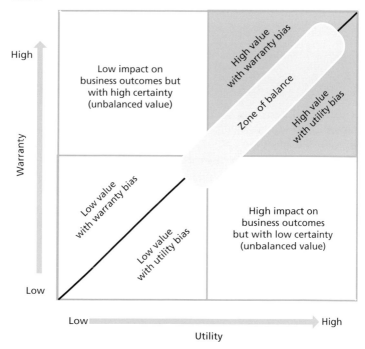

This ranking of services allows IT executives to make decisions about changing the utility and/or warranty of services based on their value to the customer and their current performance.

3.2.4.2 Communicating utility and warranty

Customers who understand the warranty and utility of a service are better able to judge its value.

Utility is usually communicated in the following terms:

- **Outcomes supported** The service provider works with the customer to ensure that both understand exactly which outcomes are achieved by specific service.
- **Cost efficiency and risk avoidance** For example, avoiding the cost of non-core or under-utilized assets.

Warranty is normally communicated in terms of:

- Service availability
- Service performance (the capacity of the service)
- Reliability (the ability of the service to perform consistently at agreed levels)
- Service continuity
- Security
- Other factors such as affordability and usability.

3.2.5 Customer assets, service assets and strategic assets

The concept of assets is defined in section 2.2. The rest of this section defines different types of assets.

3.2.5.1 Resources and capabilities

A **resource** is a type of asset used to deliver service. Resources include infrastructure, people, applications, information and money.

A **capability** is an 'intangible' type of asset which represents the ability of an organization to coordinate, deploy and control resources. Capabilities include management, knowledge and skills. Capabilities are developed over time and are enhanced by experience.

Capabilities cannot deliver value without adequate resources, and vice versa.

3.2.5.2   Business units and internal service providers

A business unit is an organizational entity, under a manager, that performs defined business activities which create value for customers in the form of goods and services. The goods or services are produced and delivered using assets, referred to as customer assets. The relationship is good as long as the customer receives value and the business unit recovers costs and receives some form of compensation or profit.

This relationship is an escalating cycle. The more a customer uses a particular service or product, the more the business unit focuses on what the customer is purchasing. The more the business unit focuses on the goods and services, the stronger their capabilities and resources become. The better the services become, the more customers are prepared to purchase them. The better the returns or cost recovery, the more the business unit will increase its investment in capabilities and resources.

Internal service providers are organizational entities, under a manager, which perform defined activities to create and deliver services that support the activities of business units. Services define the relationship between business units and their service provider counterparts.

Internal service providers use service assets to deliver services to business units. These services are designed to enhance the performance of the customer assets and/or to reduce the effect of constraints.

Just as customer assets are subject to constraints, so too are service assets. These constraints may be similar, for example limited funding or capacity. If the service provider invests in services to reduce these constraints or improve the performance, the supplier would view the service assets as customer assets and the IT services as business outcomes, and would invest in resources and capabilities to support its customer. In this way the chain of customers and service providers could extend upward and downwards.

3.2.5.3 IT service management as a strategic asset

In the context of customer and service assets, IT service management is the management of the service assets (resources and capabilities) delivering services that support the achievement of the customer's business outcomes. To the extent that IT service management is able to accomplish this, it becomes a strategic asset of the organization.

One way to achieve this is through defining, implementing and using processes. IT service management is also about the approaches, tools and management of systems and people to ensure that everything that is done in IT is linked to the achievement of a business outcome.

In Figure 3.5, an IT service provider delivers services to an internal business unit, which enables it to achieve its desired business outcomes.

Figure 3.5 How a service provider enables a business unit's outcomes

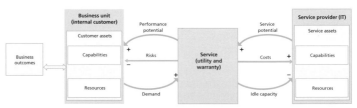

Establishing IT service management as a strategic asset does not happen immediately. It is an iterative cycle of defining value, building trust and delivering agreed services. In each cycle, the value of service management as a strategic asset is reinforced and expanded.

Figure 3.6 Growing service management into a trusted strategic asset

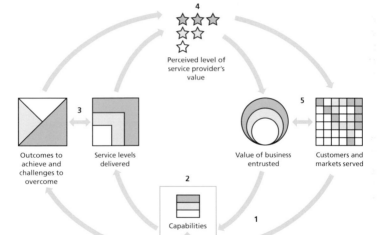

In Figure 3.6, the following steps are taken to establish IT service management as a strategic asset:

1   The cycle begins when the service provider and business have selected an opportunity. The value of this opportunity is defined in terms of outcomes and the investment required to meet them.

2   The service provider ensures that the capabilities and resources are in place to deliver the service(s).

3   These services enable the business to achieve its objectives, or overcome the defined challenge.

4   The customer perceives that the IT service provider has delivered value.

5   As a result, the customer is willing to entrust more opportunities to the service provider.

Only three iterations of the cycle are shown here, but in reality it is repeated many times over a significant time period.

3.3   SERVICE PROVIDERS

There are three main types of service provider:

- Type I – internal service provider
- Type II – shared services unit
- Type III – external service provider.

3.3.1   Type I (internal service provider)

Type I service providers are dedicated to, and often embedded within, an individual business unit. They are funded by overheads and are required to operate within the mandates of the business. Type I providers have the benefit of tight coupling with their owner-customers, and have an in-depth knowledge of the business. They are usually highly specialized, often focusing on designing, customizing and supporting specific applications, or on supporting a specific type of business process.

The general managers of business units make all key decisions such as the portfolio of services to offer, the investments in capabilities and resources, and the metrics for measuring performance and outcomes. Type I providers operate within internal market spaces. Their growth is limited by the growth of the business unit they belong to.

Competition for Type I providers is from providers outside the business unit, such as corporate business functions, offering advantages of scale, scope and autonomy. In general, service providers serving more than one customer face much lower risk of market failure: peak demand from one source can be offset by low demand from another. Duplication and waste occur when Type I providers are replicated within the enterprise.

3.3.2   Type II (shared services unit)

In Type II service providers, shared functions are consolidated into a single internal service provider supplying shared IT services to more than one business unit. These are also known as shared service units (SSUs).

This model allows a devolved governing structure under which SSUs can focus on serving business units as direct customers. SSUs can create, grow and sustain an internal market for their services, modelling themselves along the lines of service providers in the open market, spreading their costs and risks across a wider base.

SSUs are subject to comparisons with external service providers whose business practices they must emulate and whose performance they should approximate, if not exceed.

Customers of Type II are business units under a corporate parent, common stakeholders and an enterprise-level strategy. What may be sub-optimal for a particular business unit may be justified by advantages at the corporate level. Type II can offer lower prices than external service providers by leveraging corporate advantage, internal agreements and accounting policies. Operating with the autonomy of a business unit, Type II providers can make decisions outside the normal constraints by standardizing their service offerings across business units and using market-based pricing to influence demand.

However, some business units may not be satisfied with a Type II provider. If they have funding, they may attempt to compete with the Type II provider directly by creating 'rogue' or 'shadow' IT departments within the business unit. This is a governance issue, often overlooked since the service structure of the organization is not well understood. This should not be confused with a formal hybrid service provider, in which Type I and II service providers co-exist within the same organization, one focusing on shared services and the other on business-unit (BU) specific applications and services.

3.3.3 Type III (external service provider)

A Type III service provider provides IT services to external customers.

Certain business strategies are not adequately served by internal service providers such as Type I and Type II. Customers may pursue sourcing strategies requiring services from external providers. Competitive business environments often require customers to have flexible and lean structures. In such cases it is better to buy services rather than own and operate the assets.

Type III service providers have greater freedom. They can define their portfolio of services as narrowly or as broadly as they wish, and might decide not to offer certain services or engage with certain types of customer, allowing them to turn away business that might be risky.

Security is always an issue in pooled service environments. But when the environment is shared with competitors, security becomes a greater concern. This generates additional costs for Type III providers.

3.3.4 How do customers choose between types?

Customers may change from one type of service provider to another for many reasons, but each decision will require a different strategy, as illustrated in Table 3.4.

Table 3.4 Customer decisions on service provider types

From/to	Type I	Type II	Type III
Type I	Functional reorganization	Aggregation	Outsourcing
Type II	Disaggregation	Corporate reorganization	Outsourcing
Type III	Insourcing	Insourcing	Value net reconfiguration

In Table 3.4, the following strategies are indicated:

- **Functional reorganization** The business has undergone a functional reorganization, which requires a new structure of Type I service providers.
- **Corporate reorganization** A Type II service provider model is retained, but the shared services units are reorganized to provide better or more cost-effective services.

- **Value net reconfiguration** The way in which value is delivered and created by external service providers needs to be reorganized. An example of this is the emergence of cloud computing models.
- **Aggregation** Services are centralized (combined) under a single Type II provider.
- **Disaggregation** The shared services unit is decentralized (unbundled) and the service is provided by a dedicated service provider for each BU, service or activity.
- **Outsourcing** A Type III service provider is used to provide a service that was previously delivered by an internal service provider.
- **Insourcing** An internal service provider begins providing a service that was previously provided by an external service provider.

3.4   HOW TO DEFINE SERVICES

These steps may vary between organizations, and are typically carried out as part of the service portfolio management process.

3.4.1   Step 1 – Define the market and identify customers

The first step is to understand the market in which the service provider operates. For example:

- A Type I service provider will typically only serve one business unit.
- A Type II service provider's market will consist of several business units. They will not typically define and provide IT services outside the organization.
- A Type III service provider cannot provide limitless services to every market. They typically provide a generic service to several markets or specialized service(s) to a single market.

3.4.2   Step 2 – Understand the customer

Understanding the customer involves understanding:

■ **Desired business outcomes** Customers use their assets to achieve specific outcomes. Understanding these outcomes will help the service provider to define warranty and utility of their services, and to prioritize service needs.

■ **Customer assets** Services enable and support the performance of assets the customer uses to achieve business outcomes. Therefore, it is necessary to understand the linkage between the service and the customer assets.

■ **Constraints** Every customer asset is limited by some form of constraint – a lack of funding, regulations etc. Understanding constraints will enable the service provider to define boundaries for the service.

■ **How value will be perceived and measured** Customers always measure performance, quality and value. The service provider must understand how the customer measures the service – even if the service provider is not able to measure the service in the same way.

3.4.3   Step 3 – Quantify the outcomes

In this step the service provider works with the customer to identify their desired outcomes.

Understanding how services impact outcomes, and therefore what type and level of service is needed, requires the service provider to map services and outcomes. Any outcome that is not well supported is an opportunity for the service provider. It is important to review achievement of outcomes regularly, to ensure that the service provider is not missing an opportunity and that current outcomes are being delivered.

3.4.4 Step 4 – Classify and visualize the service

Every service is unique, but many have similar characteristics. If a new service shares characteristics with an existing one, it is easier to determine what it will take to deliver the service.

Classifying services and representing them visually helps to identify whether a new requirement fits within the current strategy, or whether it represents an expansion. It might also assist the service provider in deciding not to invest in a service that moves them away from their strategy.

The following areas should be visually represented:

■ The link between service assets and customer assets (i.e. what resources and capabilities do we possess, and what are we using them for?)
■ Do we have a particular strength?
  – Are there specific resources being used for existing services that could be used for other services (e.g. information or applications)? This is sometimes called an asset-based service strategy.
  – Are there specific capabilities that could be used for additional services (e.g. knowledge, management)? This is sometimes called a utility-based service strategy.
■ Can we demonstrate where value is created today, and how that could be leveraged in the future? This is sometimes referred to as visualizing value-creating patterns.

3.4.5 Step 5 – Understand the opportunities (market spaces)

Each customer has a number of requirements, and each service provider has a number of competencies; the intersections between the two are called market spaces. The market space identifies possible services that an IT service provider may wish to deliver.

More formally, market spaces are opportunities that an IT service provider could exploit to meet the business needs of customers. A market space is defined by a set of business outcomes, which can be facilitated by a service. If a service provider can deliver a service to meet those outcomes, this represents an opportunity.

3.4.6   Step 6 – Define services based on outcomes

An outcome-based definition of services ensures that managers plan and execute all aspects of service management from the perspective of what is valuable to the customer. This approach not only creates value for customers but also captures value for the service provider.

The following aspects need to be considered:

- Does the service meet a desired outcome?
- Does the service reduce the impact of a constraint on the customer?
- What elements of utility should be included (i.e. what does the service do?)
- What elements of warranty should be included (i.e. how does the service perform?)
- How does the customer measure the value of the service?

3.4.7   Step 7 – Service models

A service model shows how service assets interact with customer assets to create value. Service models describe the structure of a service (how the configuration items fit together) and the dynamics of the service (activities, flow of resources and interactions). A service model can be used as a template or blueprint for multiple services.

Service models can take many forms, from a simple chart showing the components and dependencies, to a complex analytical model analysing the dynamics of a service under different configurations and demand patterns.

A service model is not a design. It is a list or diagram of items that will deliver the service, and also shows how these items are related and how they are used by the service.

3.4.8   Step 8 – Define service units and packages

Although some services are simple, delivered in one way to one type of customer, many are complex. The same type of service may be delivered in different ways to different customers, or multiple services may be combined to achieve a single outcome. The ability to combine components in different ways for different customers allows the service provider to be flexible, yet keep costs lower.

A service package is a collection of two or more services combined to offer a solution to a specific customer need or to underpin specific business outcomes. Service packages can consist of a combination of core, enabling and enhancing services (see section 3.2.2.4). A service package does not need to have all three types of service – it only needs more than one service of any type.

Characteristics of service packages include:

- Service packages can consist of multiple services of any type (core, enabling and/or enhancing).
- Service packages can include other service packages.
- A service package can be offered with options – e.g. a mobile telephone company may offer a different number of monthly call minutes and data quantity for each service package.

- Service packages may consist of a number of services, some of which are optional.
- In cloud computing, customers are able to choose their own combination of services and service levels – thus creating their own service packages.
- Services may be packaged around predefined demographic groups and marketed to those groups. This is called segmentation, and makes it easier for the service provider to standardize services, facilitating distribution and support and optimizing costs.

3.5   STRATEGIES FOR CUSTOMER SATISFACTION

Customers should feel satisfied with the level of service they receive and confident in the ability of the service provider to continue providing that service – or even improving it over time. Customer expectations are constantly shifting, and service providers who do not track this will soon lose business.

Figure 3.7 illustrates the Kano model of customer perceptions of utility, showing a relationship between the level of fulfilment of customer needs that a service offers, and the level of satisfaction that a customer feels.

The Kano model shows three different types of factors involved in customer satisfaction:

- **Basic factors** Service features that must be in place for the customer to receive the service. Basic factors are not responsible for high levels of satisfaction, unless they alone fulfil the customer's requirements completely.
- **Performance factors** These enable a customer to get more of something that they need, or a higher level of service quality. The more a customer wants, the more they will expect to pay, and thus the greater value that each factor must contribute.

Figure 3.7 Perceptions of utility and customer satisfaction

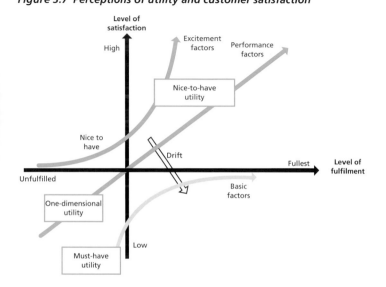

- ■ **Excitement factors** Generous attributes of a service that customers do not expect, so when they are offered (within reason) they cause higher satisfaction levels. These factors are not essential to the service, and are also referred to as a 'nice-to-have utility'. If delivered consistently, customers will come to expect these as basic, thus causing a drift in expectations.

A well-designed service provides the appropriate combination of basic, performance and excitement attributes.

3.6   SERVICE ECONOMICS

Service economics relate to the balance between the cost of providing services, the value of the outcomes attained and the returns that the service provider achieves.

Figure 3.8 Service economic dynamics for internal service providers

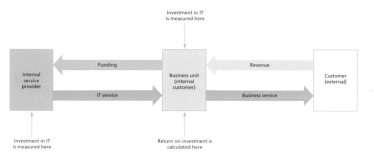

Figure 3.8 illustrates typical dynamics involved in relationships between internal suppliers, business units and external customers. The business unit offers business services to an external customer. In return for those services the customer pays the business unit money (revenue). The business unit uses an IT service from the internal service provider and funds the service (this is seen as a cost to the business unit). The business unit can calculate the value of the IT service by comparing the revenue they received with the funding they gave to the service provider. Thus, value – as well as increases in value or return on investment (ROI) – can only be calculated at the business unit.

If the organization is delivering IT services to external customers, the ROI of the services can be measured directly.

Service economics relies on five main areas:

- **Service portfolio management** The process that defines the outcomes which the business desires to achieve, and the services that will be used to achieve them. This is covered in more detail in section 4.2 of this publication.
- **Financial management for IT services** The process which calculates, forecasts and tracks costs and income related to services. This is covered in more detail in section 4.3 of this publication.
- **Return on investment** (ROI) A measurement of the expected or actual benefit of an investment.
- **Business impact analysis** (BIA) This allows an organization to establish relative priorities of services, based on their effect on the business if they were not available.
- **Demand management** A process that works to gear IT resources to meet the changing demands of business. Changes in demand reflect a potential change to the value of services, and their ability to enable the business to meet its objectives.

3.6.1   Return on investment

In service management, ROI is used as a measure of the ability to use assets to generate additional value.

A very simple ROI calculation would look something like the following:

$$ROI = \frac{\text{Increase in profit resulting from the service}}{\text{Total investment in the service}}$$

Since this calculation does not always show the full range of tangible and intangible benefits of an investment, most organizations use additional metrics to measure ROI. The most common are:

- **Business case** A decision support and planning tool that projects the likely consequences of a business action. These can include qualitative and quantitative dimensions related to business objectives and potential business impact.
- **Pre-programme ROI** Capital budgeting is the commitment of funds now to receive a return in the future in the form of additional cash inflows or reduced cash outflows. ROI calculations take into account the relative value of the investment over a longer period of time. There are two types of capital-budgeting decisions:
  - **Screening decisions** Usually use net present value (NPV) to determine whether an initiative surpasses a predetermined return rate over time
  - **Preference decisions** Compare several initiatives using an internal rate of return (IRR) calculation.
- **Post-programme ROI** Evaluate the achieved returns on an investment that has already been made.

3.6.2 Business impact analysis

Business impact analysis (BIA) is used to evaluate the relative value of services. BIA examines what would happen if the service was unavailable, or only partially available, over different periods of time. This method allows the customer to express the value of the service in terms that are meaningful to it – both financial and non-financial.

3.7 SOURCING STRATEGY

Sourcing is about analysing how best to source and deploy the resources and capabilities required to deliver outcomes to customers. A service strategy should enhance an organization's strengths and core competencies. As organizations seek to improve their performance, they should consider which competencies are essential and know when to extend their capabilities by partnering inside or outside their enterprise.

Outsourcing moves a value-creating activity outside the organization where it is performed by another company. The assessment is whether the extra value generated from performing an activity inside the organization outweighs the costs of managing it internally. This decision can change over time.

3.7.1   Deciding what to source

Deciding to outsource is about finding ways to improve competitive differentiation by redeploying resources and capabilities that are only peripheral to the organization's core strategy.

3.7.2   Sourcing structures

The organization should adopt a formal governance approach to manage outsourced services and assure the delivery of value. This includes planning for organizational change and documenting how decisions on services are made. The selection of a sourcing structure should be balanced with acceptable risks and levels of control.

Table 3.5 outlines major options for sourcing structures.

3.7.3   Multi-vendor sourcing

Sourcing services from multiple providers has become the norm, delivering benefits and gaining increasing support. The organization maintains a strong relationship with each provider, spreading the risk and reducing costs.

Table 3.5 Main sourcing structures (delivery strategies)

Sourcing strategy	Description
Insourcing	Utilizes internal organizational resources in the design, development, transition, maintenance, operation and/or support of new, changed or revised services.
Outsourcing	Utilizes the resources of external organizations in a formal arrangement to provide a well-defined portion of a service's design, development, maintenance, operations and/or support.
Co-sourcing or multi-sourcing	Often a combination of insourcing and outsourcing. A number of external organizations may work together to design, develop, transition, maintain, operate and/or support a portion of a service.
Partnership	Formal arrangements between two or more organizations to work together to design, develop, transition, maintain, operate and/or support IT service(s). The focus here is on strategic partnerships that leverage critical expertise or market opportunities.

Table continues

Table 3.5 *continued*

Sourcing strategy	Description
Business process outsourcing (BPO)	The increasing trend of relocating entire business functions using formal arrangements where one organization provides and manages another organization's entire business process(es) or function(s) in a low-cost location. Common examples are accounting, payroll and call-centre operations.
Application service provision	Outsourcing to an application service provider (ASP) organization that will provide shared computer-based services over a network from the service provider's premises. Such applications are sometimes referred to as on-demand software/applications. Through ASPs, complexities and costs of shared software can be reduced and offered to organizations that could otherwise not justify the investment.

Table continues

Table 3.5 *continued*

Sourcing strategy	Description
Knowledge process outsourcing (KPO)	KPO organizations provide domain-based processes and business expertise rather than just process expertise. The organization is not only required to execute a process, but also to make low-level decisions based on knowledge of local conditions or industry-specific information. For example, outsourcing of credit risk assessment, where the outsourcing organization has historical information that it has analysed to create knowledge which enables it to provide a service. For every credit card company to collect and analyse this data for itself would not be as cost-effective as using KPO.
'Cloud'	Cloud service providers offer specific predefined services, usually on demand. Services are normally standard, but can be customized to a specific organization if there is enough demand. Cloud services can be offered internally, but generally refer to outsourced service provision.
Multi-vendor sourcing	This involves sourcing services from various vendors, often representing different sourcing options from the above.

However, managing several vendors and contracts can be challenging. It should also be noted that each provider may represent a different type of sourcing option.

3.7.4   Service provider interfaces

A service provider interface (SPI) is a formally defined reference point, which identifies some interaction between a service provider and a user, customer, process or one or more suppliers. SPIs ensure that multiple parties in a business relationship have the same points of reference for defining, delivering and reporting services. SPIs help coordinate end-to-end management of critical services.

3.8   SERVICE STRUCTURES IN THE VALUE NETWORK

Linear models are inadequate for describing the complexities of value for service management, often treating information as a supporting element rather than a source of value.

An effective service provider will view service management as patterns of collaborative exchanges, rather than an assembly line. From a systems-thinking perspective it is more useful to regard service management as a value network or net.

A value network is a web of relationships that generates tangible and intangible value through complex dynamic exchanges between two or more organizations. The increasingly low cost of information enables IT executives to use this approach more freely.

Value net diagrams are tools for service analysis, rather than flow charts for work instructions. They show what an organization does, how it is done and for whom, helping to simplify the way the organization works, making it more efficient. They need not be overly complex to be useful.

3.9   GOVERNANCE

Governance is the single overarching area that ties IT and the business together, and services are one way of ensuring that the organization is able to execute that governance. Governance defines the common directions, policies and rules that the business and IT use to conduct business.

Many IT service management strategies fail because they focus on how they would like the organization to work instead of working within existing governance structures.

Definition: governance

Ensures that policies and strategy are actually implemented, and that required processes are correctly followed. Governance includes defining roles and responsibilities, measuring and reporting, and taking actions to resolve any issues identified.

The standard for corporate governance of IT is ISO/IEC 38500. Governance is performed by governors (usually a board of directors). Governors are concerned with ensuring that the organization adheres to rules and policies; but further, that the desired end results are being achieved.

Management is performed by executives and people who report to them. Their job is to execute the rules, processes and operations of the organization according to the governance policies, and to achieve the strategies defined by the governors. Managers coordinate and control the work that is required to meet the strategy, within the defined policies and rules. The executives ensure that governance and management are aligned.

Key activities of governance are:

- Setting the strategy policies and plans
- Ongoing evaluation of the organization's performance and environment
- Directing management to achieve the strategy through implementation of plans using the approved policies
- Monitoring the organization to ensure that governance is being fulfilled.

3.10   THE SERVICE MANAGEMENT SYSTEM

Governance works to apply a consistently managed approach at all levels of the organization. Areas of specialization and processes within the organization are controlled by management systems.

A service management system (SMS) is used to direct and control service management activities to enable effective implementation and management of services. Processes are established and continually improved to support delivery of service management.

Definition: management system (taken from ISO 9001)

A system to establish policy and objectives and to achieve those objectives.

A system can be further defined as a set of processes, technology and people working cohesively to achieve a set of common goals. Note that the management system of an organization can include different management systems, such as a quality management system, a financial management system or an environmental management system.

The SMS includes all service management strategies, policies, objectives, plans, processes, documentation and resources required to deliver services to customers. It also identifies the organizational structure, authorities, roles and responsibilities associated with the oversight of service management processes.

3.11   IT SERVICE STRATEGY AND ENTERPRISE ARCHITECTURE

Enterprise architecture describes an organization's enterprise and associated components. It covers the organizational relationship with systems, sub-systems and external environments along with their interdependencies. Enterprise architecture also sets out the relationship with enterprise goals, business functions, business processes, roles, organizational structures, business information, software applications and computer systems – and how these interoperate to ensure the viability and growth of the organization.

Enterprise architecture injects valuable intelligence into service strategy with clear definitions of business processes and solid engineering-design principles. Enterprise architecture also plays a key role in the creation, use, maintenance and modelling of a reusable set of architectures for the organization. These domains might include business architecture, information architecture, technology architecture, governance architecture and others. IT and service strategy development/maintenance should include representation from enterprise architecture to ensure seamless integration and alignment across an organization's enterprise and associated components. Development and maintenance of this is typically handled by the IT steering committee.

3.12   APPLICATION DEVELOPMENT

Application development teams should maintain alignment with service strategy by incorporating it into product line strategies and internal development efforts. Application development plans should be aligned to support service and IT strategy. In a sense, the application development strategy will have its own four Ps of strategy (perspective, position, plans and patterns) but it derives overall direction from the service and IT strategy. This can also play a key role in helping the organization achieve an appropriate balance of innovation versus operations.

3.13   SERVICE STRATEGY INPUTS AND OUTPUTS

The main inputs to service strategy are information and feedback for business cases, requirements and feedback for strategies and plans, financial reports, service reports, dashboards and outputs of review meetings.

The main outputs from service strategy are the vision and mission, strategies and strategic plans, the service portfolio, change proposals and financial information.

4 Service strategy processes

4.1 STRATEGY MANAGEMENT FOR IT SERVICES

4.1.1 Purpose and objectives

Strategy management for IT services ensures that the strategy is defined, maintained and achieves its purpose. The purpose of strategy management is to define and maintain the service provider's perspective, position, plans and patterns relative to the organization's enterprise strategy.

The major objectives of strategy management for IT services are to:

- Analyse internal and external environments to identify opportunities that will benefit the organization.
- Identify constraints that might prevent the achievement of business outcomes or delivery of services, and define how those constraints could be managed.
- Agree the service provider's perspective and review regularly to produce a clear statement of the vision and mission of the service provider.
- Establish the position of the service provider, defining which services will be delivered to which market spaces, and how to maintain a competitive advantage.
- Produce and maintain strategy-planning documents.
- Ensure that strategic plans have been translated into tactical and operational plans for each organizational unit that is expected to deliver on the strategy.
- Manage changes to strategies and related documents, ensuring that they keep pace with changes to internal and external environments.

4.1.2   Scope

The overall strategy of an organization will be broken down into a strategy for each unit of the business, as illustrated in Figure 4.1 (where manufacturing is used as an example of another business unit). There are likely to be several strategies within each organization; strategy management for the enterprise has to ensure that these are linked and consistent. Strategy management for IT services guarantees that the services and the way they are managed support the overall strategy of the enterprise.

Figure 4.1 Enterprise strategy and the strategy of business units

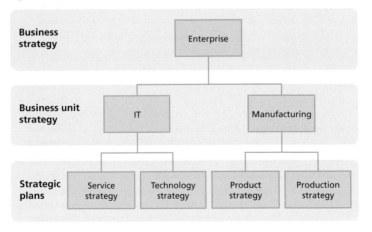

The IT strategy (and therefore also the strategy for IT services) is derived from the business strategy, and provides validation of that strategy. The IT strategy can determine whether a strategic objective is technologically possible, and what investment is required to meet that objective.

A service strategy is not the same as an ITSM strategy – which is really a tactical plan. The difference is:

- **Service strategy** The strategy that a service provider will follow to define and execute services which meet a customer's business objectives. For an IT service provider the service strategy is a subset of the IT strategy.
- **IT service management strategy** The plan for identifying, implementing and executing processes used to manage services. In an IT service provider, the ITSM strategy is a subset of the service strategy.

4.1.3   Value to business

Without a strategy the organization is only able to react to demands placed by stakeholders, with little ability to assess each demand and its impact on the organization. A well-defined and managed strategy ensures that resources and capabilities are aligned to achieving business outcomes, and that investments match the organization's intended development and growth.

Strategy management for IT services ensures that the service provider has appropriate services in its service portfolio, that all services have a clear purpose, and that everyone in the service provider organization knows their role in achieving that purpose. Strategy management for IT services encourages appropriate investment, aligned to business priorities, resulting in one or more of:

- Cost savings, since investments and expenditure are matched to achievement of validated business objectives
- Increased levels of investment for key projects or service improvements
- Shifting investment priorities. The service provider can ensure that its efforts and budget are spent on areas with the highest level of business impact.

Strategy management for IT services enables customers to articulate their business priorities in a way that is understandable to the service provider.

4.1.4 Policies, principles and basic concepts

If the organization is an external service provider with a core business of providing services, the service strategy will be the central component of the enterprise strategy.

In internal service providers, the service strategy supports the overall enterprise strategy, and provides a tactical plan for the internal service provider. In other words, while the IT strategy is strategic to the IT department, the board of directors would consider it to be tactical. It is therefore vital that the IT strategy is defined in terms of the organization's overall strategy.

4.1.5 Process activities, methods and techniques

The process for strategy management is illustrated in Figure 4.2 and described below.

4.1.5.1 Strategic assessment

The strategic assessment analyses the internal and external environment, and arrives at objectives which are used to define the strategy. Strategic assessment consists of five major activities:

Figure 4.2 The strategy management process

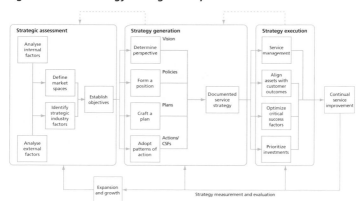

■ **Analyse the internal environment** Identify the service provider's strengths and weaknesses through an internal analysis. This will help to define the strategy by identifying which strengths can be leveraged, and which weaknesses need to be strengthened.

■ **Analyse the external environment** The external analysis focuses on opportunities and threats, especially how they will develop in the future. The aim is to identify which opportunities to exploit and which threats to defend against.

■ **Define market spaces** Service providers analyse their business potential based on unserved or under-served market spaces. This identifies opportunities with current and prospective customers. It also prioritizes investments in service assets based on their potential to serve market spaces of interest.

When the strategy is generated, the service provider will use this information to decide whether to continue servicing existing market spaces and, if so, whether any changes are needed to ensure successful retention of the market space.

■ **Identify strategic industry factors** A strategic industry factor is any requirement that a service provider must meet in order to participate in a particular industry. These could be influenced by customer needs, business trends, competition, regulatory environment, suppliers, standards, industry best practices and technologies.

Strategic industry factors determine whether the service provider can compete effectively in a market space. They also help to determine where the service provider should invest more in a particular market space, or offer a broader (or narrower) range of services to existing customer(s). Strategic industry factors have the following general characteristics:

- They are defined in terms of capabilities and resources.
- They are proven to be key determinants of success by industry leaders.
- They are defined by market space levels, not peculiar to any one firm.
- They are the basis for competition among rivals.
- They change over time, so they are dynamic not static.
- They usually require significant investment and time to develop.

■ **Establish objectives** Objectives articulate what the service provider hopes to achieve as the result of pursuing a strategy. Meaningful objectives are based on outcomes customers desire to achieve. Objectives help the service provider determine how best to satisfy these outcomes.

Characteristics of good objectives include:

- 'SMART' objectives – specific, measurable, achievable, relevant, time-bound.
- There should not be too many objectives, and they should be prioritized into primary and secondary objectives.
- They should be agreed by all stakeholders.
- Objectives are only met when all parties agree that they have been met.

4.1.5.2 Strategy generation, evaluation and selection

Determine perspective

Perspective defines overall direction, values, beliefs and purpose, and – at a high level – how to achieve these. The most common forms of perspective are vision and mission statements.

A good perspective has four main purposes:

- To clarify the direction of the service provider
- To motivate people to take action that moves the organization to make the vision reality
- To coordinate the actions of different people or groups
- To represent the view of senior management as they direct the organization towards its overall objectives.

Perspective does not just articulate the objectives and core business of the organization, but it also forms the basis for its culture. The perspective provides a basis for setting common goals throughout the organization and ensuring that appropriate actions and behaviour are encouraged at all levels.

Form a position

The strategic position defines how the service provider will be differentiated from other service providers. The position also determines how assets are used.

Apart from the cost and quality of services, there are four broad types of positioning:

- **Variety-based positioning** The service provider delivers a narrow catalogue of services to a variety of customers. Service assets are specialized, and the service provider does not attempt to meet all the needs of a particular customer or customer segment.
- **Needs-based positioning ('customer intimacy')** The service provider delivers a broad range of services to meet the needs of an individual customer or type of customer. Service providers differentiate themselves by performing exceptionally well in meeting most of the needs of a particular customer or segment.
- **Access-based positioning** The service provider offers a range of services to multiple customers who have something in common other than being in the same industry segment. This could be location, scale or structure.
- **Demand-based positioning** This contains features of both variety- and needs-based positioning. It offers a broad range of services to a potentially unlimited number of customers. One example is 'cloud' services. In this positioning, companies use IT to engage directly with a huge variety of customers and individual consumers. There is a range of service options, which can be combined in any number of service packages – all driven by the consumer directly.

Once a position has been determined, it can be tested by asking the following questions:

- Does it guide the organization in making decisions between competing resource and capability investments?
- Does it help managers test the appropriateness of a particular course of action?

- Does it set clear boundaries within which staff should and should not operate?
- Does it allow freedom to experiment within these constraints?

Craft a plan

The plan is a deliberate course of action towards strategic objectives and describes how the organization will move from one point to another within a specific scenario. The strategy is often a collection of plans, each aimed at achieving a specific set of objectives, or a specific position.

Adopt patterns of action

A pattern of action is how an organization works. Formal hierarchies show one view of the organization, but interactions between these hierarchies, the exchange of information, the handover of units of work and the exchange of money all contribute to a network of activity that gets things done. Patterns are manifested in management systems, organizational structures, policies, processes, procedures, budgets etc.

Patterns of action work in two ways. Firstly, the strategy defines patterns that executives believe will be efficient and effective in achieving objectives. Secondly, as the organization and its environment change, the strategy should be adapted and strengthened. People find better ways to do things, see new opportunities and detect new customer needs or innovative technologies. Strategy takes this into account and evolves.

When patterns of action are formalized, they are placed under configuration management so they can be stabilized, standardized and improved. Each formal pattern of action becomes a baseline from which improvements can be made.

In this way service management can be viewed as an adaptive network of patterns through which strategic objectives are realized.

4.1.5.3   Strategy execution

The service strategy is executed through the service lifecycle. More detailed tactical plans describe approaches and methods that will be used to achieve the strategy in each stage of the lifecycle. If a strategy answers the question 'where are we going?' then tactics answer the question 'how will we get there?'

Other service management processes

Other service management processes provide a management system that formalizes how the service provider will manage services.

The strategy defines a number of opportunities. Other service management processes define the services to meet those opportunities. Service management processes also manage the activities, tools and people that deliver and support the services.

Align assets with customer outcomes

The service provider needs to communicate what services are being provided, and to which customers. The service portfolio contains this information, details of the business outcomes that each service enables, and it also identifies who the service owner is and who is involved in delivering and supporting the service.

The service provider needs to decide how services will be delivered. Architecture and service models are produced; service management processes work together to define the optimal design and configuration of the service assets. The aim is to increase productive use of assets and optimize costs.

Optimize critical success factors

The core ITIL publications describe the critical success factors (CSFs) that are required for each process and each stage of the lifecycle. *ITIL Service Strategy* defines an additional level of CSFs. These relate to areas that must be in place for the organization to compete in a specific industry or market space. CSFs in this context are aspects or properties of the organization which enable them to achieve the strategic industry factors identified in the strategy assessment.

In this stage of strategy execution the organization, services, processes, skills, tools etc. are compared with the strategic industry factors, and any gaps identified. If the organization is not positioned to meet a strategic industry factor, a project will be initiated to implement the critical success factors.

Prioritize investments

Service portfolio management ensures that every proposed new service, or strategic change to a service, is analysed to determine the investment required and the proposed return on investment. It also analyses whether customers are under- or over-served in terms of utility and warranty for each service. This information is used to prioritize investments. The project management office (PMO) will ensure that this is done for any projects proposed as part of strategy execution. Service portfolio management will also identify whether any services are dependent on the proposed projects, ensuring that any decision to cancel a project is made with full understanding of the impact. The strategy may be amended after reviewing the detailed investment analysis, if there is insufficient funding, or because the anticipated return does not support the investment.

4.1.5.4 Measurement and evaluation

This stage of strategy management is performed by a number of different areas, including:

- **Customers and users** Who are often the first to determine whether a strategy is being achieved or not.
- **Service management processes** If each process has been designed to execute and enable the strategy of the organization, its metrics can be used to measure the effectiveness of the strategy.
- **Continual service improvement** Continual measurement of the performance of services and service management will show any deviation from forecast results.
- **The organization's executives** Executives need a dashboard to indicate the organization's performance relative to its strategy.

Continual service improvement

Continual service improvement (CSI) measures and evaluates the achievement of strategy over time. This contributes to strategy measurement and evaluation in two main ways.

Firstly, CSI identifies areas that are not performing as expected, and provides feedback into strategy generation and execution phases of the process. Secondly, CSI sets the baseline for the next round of strategy assessments.

Expansion and growth

As the organization achieves its strategy, it gets better at delivering services to existing market spaces. This raises questions such as: *'Can we provide the same services to new customers?'*, *'Can we provide new services to existing customers?'* and *'Can we deliver new services to new customers?'*

Organizations may decide to expand into adjacent market spaces or to meet the needs of an existing market space more comprehensively.

4.1.5.5   Strategy management for internal IT service providers

Internal IT departments often make the mistake of thinking that they do not play a strategic role in the organization and confining their activities to tactical planning and execution.

However, IT is a strategic part of most businesses, and it is important that the IT department strategy is aligned with the business strategy. This is done in two ways:

- Ensuring that the IT strategy is closely linked to the business strategy
- Following the steps set out earlier in section 4.1.5 to define the IT strategy, but using a narrower scope, specific inputs and defined parameters.

4.1.6   Triggers, inputs, outputs and interfaces

Triggers for strategy management for IT services include:

- **Annual planning cycles** To review and plan on an annual basis
- **New business opportunity** To analyse, set objectives, perspectives, positions, plans and patterns for new business or service opportunities
- **Changes to internal or external environments** To assess the impact of environmental changes on the existing strategic and tactical plans
- **Mergers or acquisitions** These will trigger detailed analysis and definition of the strategy for the new organization.

Inputs to strategy management for IT services include:

- Existing plans
- Research on aspects of the environment by specialized research organizations
- Vendor strategies and product roadmaps
- Customer interviews and strategic plans
- Service portfolio
- Service reports
- Audit reports that indicate compliance with (or deviation from) the organization's strategy.

Outputs of strategy management for IT services include:

- Strategic and tactical plans
- Strategy review schedules and documentation
- Mission and vision statements
- Policies that show how the plans should be executed, how services will be designed, transitioned, operated and improved
- Requirements for new services, input into which services need to be changed, documentation of what business outcomes need to be met and how services will accomplish this.

The interfaces of strategy management for IT services are such that it:

- Interfaces and directs all service management processes, either directly or indirectly.
- Provides the guidelines and framework within which the service portfolio will be defined and managed.
- Provides input to financial management indicating what types of returns are required and where investments should be made. Financial management provides information and

tools enabling strategy management for IT services to prioritize actions and plans.

■ Provides input to service design. Identifies policies that must be considered when designing services, constraints on the design teams, and prioritization of work. Service design processes feed back into strategy management for IT services to enable measurement and evaluation of services being designed.

■ Enables service transition to prioritize and evaluate services so that they meet the strategic intent and requirements.

■ Provides direction for operational execution of strategic priorities. Operational tools and processes must be aligned to strategic objectives and desired business outcomes. Monitoring of operational environments indicates the effectiveness of the strategy.

■ Works with continual service improvement to evaluate whether the strategy has been executed effectively, and whether it has met its objectives.

4.1.7   Critical success factors and key performance indicators

Examples of CSFs and key performance indicators (KPIs) for strategy management for IT services include:

■ **CSF** The service provider has a clear understanding of its perspective, and it is reviewed regularly to ensure ongoing relevance
  – **KPI** Vision and mission statements have been defined and all staff members trained on what these mean in terms of their roles and jobs within the organization

■ **CSF** The service provider has a clear understanding of how it positions itself to ensure competitive advantage
  – **KPI** Every strategic and tactical plan contains a statement of how the contents of the plan support the competitive advantage of the service provider.

Challenges for strategy management for IT services include:

- The process being conducted at the wrong level in the organization
- Lack of accurate information about the external environment
- Lack of support by stakeholders
- Lack of appropriate tools
- Operational targets needing to be matched to strategic objectives.

Risks to strategy management for IT services include:

- A flawed governance model
- Short-term priorities overriding the directives of the strategy
- Strategic decisions being taken using incomplete information about internal or external environments, or details that are incorrect or misleading.
- Strategies being seen as an exercise that happens once a year with no bearing on what happens for the rest of the year.

4.2 SERVICE PORTFOLIO MANAGEMENT

4.2.1 Purpose and objectives

The purpose of service portfolio management is to ensure that the service provider has the right mix of services to balance the investment in IT with the ability to meet business outcomes. It tracks the investment in services throughout their lifecycle and works with other service management processes to ensure that the appropriate returns are being achieved. It therefore describes the provider's services in terms of business value.

The objectives of service portfolio management are to:

- Decide which services enter the service portfolio

- Maintain the definitive portfolio of services, articulating the business needs each service meets and the business outcomes it supports
- Provide a mechanism to evaluate how services enable the organization to achieve its strategy, and to respond to changes in the internal or external environments
- Control which services are offered, under what conditions and at what level of investment
- Track investment in services throughout their lifecycle
- Analyse which services are no longer viable and when they should be retired.

4.2.2 Scope

The scope of service portfolio management is all the services a service provider plans to deliver, those currently delivered and those that have been withdrawn from service.

4.2.3 Value to business

Service portfolio management enables the business to make sound decisions about investments. Services are implemented only if there is a good business case demonstrating a clear return on investment.

Customers are able to understand exactly what the service provider will deliver and under what conditions, enabling them to decide whether the service is a good investment, and to evaluate additional opportunities that the service will open. Thus service portfolio management can be a tool for innovation.

4.2.4 Policies, principles and basic concepts

4.2.4.1 The service portfolio

The service portfolio represents the commitments and investments made by a service provider across all customers and market spaces. It describes present commitments, new service development and ongoing service improvement plans.

The service portfolio represents all the resources presently engaged or being released in various stages of the service lifecycle. It should have the right mix of services in the pipeline and catalogue to secure the financial viability of the service provider, since the service catalogue is the only part of the portfolio that lists services that recover costs or earn profits.

Figure 4.3 The service portfolio

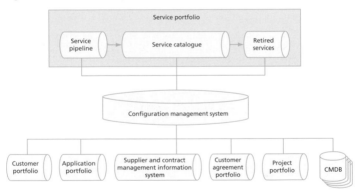

The service portfolio consists of three components (as illustrated in Figure 4.3):

- **Service pipeline** The service pipeline is a database or structured document listing all services that are under consideration or development, but are not yet available to customers. It also includes any major investment opportunities. The service pipeline ensures that opportunities are properly quantified in terms of investment and return.

■ **Service catalogue** The service catalogue is a database or structured document with information about all live IT services, including those available for deployment. It is the only part of the service portfolio published to customers. It identifies the linkage between service assets, services and business outcomes. This information identifies where existing services meet current business outcomes and potential gaps in the service portfolio. It also identifies the demand for a service and shows how this will be fulfilled.

■ **Retired services** The service portfolio enables a service provider to assess when a service no longer meets the objectives of the organization, or is no longer cost-effective.

The service portfolio (and especially the service catalogue) can be used to identify the demand for a service and how the service provider will fulfil the demand. Every time the business works to achieve a business outcome, it places demand on the services. Demand management identifies these patterns of business activity and how they are fulfilled by services. It can also identify the degree to which services meet the level of demand. Using the service portfolio, capacity management can identify services that are not properly supported or service assets that are under-utilized or over-utilized.

4.2.4.2 Configuration management system

The configuration management system (CMS) records and controls data about each service, configuration items (CIs) that make up services, the people and tools that support services and the relationships between them. This information is critical for making decisions about the viability of services.

4.2.4.3   Application portfolio

The application portfolio is a database or structured document used to manage applications throughout their lifecycle. It contains key attributes of all applications.

The application portfolio allows strategic service requirements and requests to be linked to applications or projects within application development. This allows development and operations teams to quantify and evaluate opportunities in the service pipeline in conjunction with one another. It also enables the organization to track investments at all stages of the service lifecycle, and enables application development and IT operations to coordinate their efforts.

4.2.4.4   Customer portfolio

The customer portfolio is a database or structured document that records all customers of the IT service provider. This is the business relationship manager's view of the customers.

Service portfolio management uses the customer portfolio to ensure that the relationship between business outcomes, customers and services is well understood.

4.2.4.5   Customer agreement portfolio

The customer agreement portfolio is a database or structured document used to manage service contracts or agreements between an IT service provider and its customers.

External service providers use the customer agreement portfolio to track contractual requirements and link them to the service portfolio and customer portfolio. Internal service providers use it to track SLAs and less formal agreements to ensure that customer expectations are met.

The customer agreement portfolio enables the service provider to identify the most stringent requirement that it must meet.

4.2.4.6   Project portfolio

The project portfolio is a database or structured document used to manage projects throughout their lifecycle.

This is important since new services, and many changes to services, are managed as projects. The project portfolio helps service portfolio management to track the status of projects, compare expenditure with expected investment, and ensure that the services are built as intended.

4.2.4.7   Service models

Service portfolio management uses service models to analyse the impact of new or changed services. A service model is defined for each service in the pipeline. Service models are also valuable in assessing which existing service assets can be used to support new services – thus increasing efficiency via the principle of 'create once, use many times'.

4.2.4.8   Service portfolio management through the service lifecycle

Although service portfolio management is a process within service strategy, it is also fundamental at every stage of the service lifecycle.

In *service design*, service portfolio management ensures that design work is prioritized according to business needs, and that there is a clear understanding of how the service will be measured by the business. Each service is clearly linked to agreed outcomes, showing how service assets will be used and identifying the performance that will be required.

Service portfolio management also provides input to the teams involved in building services, ensuring that they remain focused on the objectives, outcomes and priorities of each service. It also works with the PMO or project manager to monitor the build process to ensure that the services are built on time, to specification and to budget.

Service transition processes build and test the services that will be placed into the service catalogue. The service portfolio provides guidance on build, testing and evaluation.

Service operation processes deliver the service in the service catalogue part of the service portfolio. Service portfolio management provides an understanding of the services and how and why they are needed. This input is important for defining standard operating procedures, event management, incident management priorities and escalation procedures.

Continual service improvement evaluates whether the services in the portfolio meet the objectives and, if not, identifies solutions.

4.2.5   Process activities, methods and techniques

The activities of the service portfolio management process are illustrated in Figure 4.4 and described below.

4.2.5.1   Process initiation

New services and changes to existing services can be initiated from a range of sources and presented in various forms. The major points of process initiation are:

- **Strategy management for IT services** The process input is a strategic initiative.
- **Business relationship management** The input is in the form a customer request.

Figure 4.4 Phases of service portfolio management

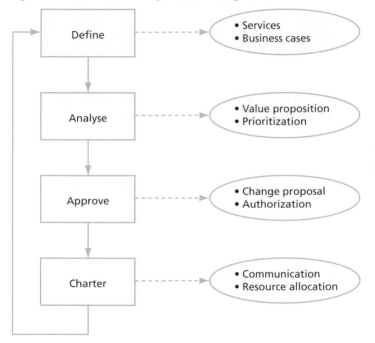

- ■ **Continual service improvement** CSI initiates three types of input using service improvement plans:
  - – Improvement to services in the portfolio
  - – New opportunities or gaps in the current portfolio
  - – Overall improvements in cost or risk mitigation.

■ **Other service management processes** The form of input is a service suggestion. Suggestions can be routed through change management, but this is not recommended if the suggestion has a significant impact on levels of investment or achievement of business outcomes.

4.2.5.2 Define

The steps for defining existing and new services differ, since existing services already exist in the service portfolio and have service models.

Defining new services involves the following activities:

■ **Define service, customers and business outcomes** Defines customer needs, required utility and warranty, and anticipated investment. This is not a detailed architecture for the service (which is done during service design).
■ **Define service model** Provides a high-level view of all components of the service and how they fit together.

The following activities are involved in defining changes to existing services:

■ **Define impact on service portfolio** Evaluates the impact on the existing utility, warranty and investment of the service, and any linked services. This step also defines how the change will impact business outcomes, and highlights necessary investment.
■ **Define impact on service model** Identifies the impact on the service model, including the service dynamics, data flows, components and constraints.

4.2.5.3 Analyse

The analysis links each service to the service strategy and articulates how the perspective, position, plans and patterns will be translated into actual services.

This requires input from many areas. Some organizations use a pool of senior architects and managers (the service architecture board – SAB) to evaluate each service. This group also validates the analysis work and ensures that the change proposal is properly prepared.

Service portfolio review

This is an ongoing activity within service portfolio management, which determines whether services still meet their objectives, and whether they remain appropriate for the strategy. The review also ensures that services are properly defined, analysed, approved and chartered.

Analyse investments, value and priorities

Service portfolio management works with financial management for IT services to map service assets to services to business outcomes; and then to assess the investment needed and the anticipated ROI. This information is input into service design, transition and operation to prioritize work.

Articulate value proposition

Once investment analysis and prioritization have been completed, the results are documented in a business case, which describes the opportunity and what the service is expected to achieve.

4.2.5.4   Approve

The following decisions and actions are taken here:

■   **Is the service or change feasible?** Once the value proposition has been articulated and a business case documented, service portfolio management works with customers and executives to decide whether the service is feasible. It will not be feasible if it cannot achieve required business outcomes, or if the investment is too high for the estimated return.

■ **Change proposal** Details of the new service or changes have not yet been defined in sufficient detail for a request for change (RFC). Instead, service portfolio management submits a change proposal, allowing design teams to spend money and prioritize resources in advance of a final decision.

■ **Change management** The change proposal is treated similarly to an RFC, except that the activity is focused on investigating what the new or changed service will look like and what it will take to design, build and deploy it. The objective is to obtain sufficient information to decide whether or not the service is feasible.

■ **Change proposal approved?** If the change proposal is approved, service portfolio management will use feedback from change management to draft a service charter. If it is rejected, service portfolio management will notify stakeholders and update the status in the service portfolio.

4.2.5.5   Charter

'Charter' has two meanings, both of which are relevant here:

■ A verb indicating that the new or changed service has been commissioned by the customer or business executives
■ A noun referring to a document which authorizes work to meet defined objectives, outputs, schedules and expenditure. In service portfolio management, services are chartered using a service charter.

The service charter ensures that all stakeholders have a common understanding of what will be built, the deadline and the cost. The use of the word 'charter' signifies that the changes will be managed using a project management approach, which in larger organizations will be managed using a project management office (PMO).

Major activities during the charter stage of the process are to:

- Communicate with stakeholders
- Monitor the service through service design and transition
- Check to ensure that the service is successful.

4.2.5.6   Review

Three additional activities related to reviewing the services and service portfolio are performed as part of the service portfolio management process. These are:

- **Review the success of the service** Similar to the post-implementation review in change management, but broader in scope. The question here is whether the service has met the requirements of the strategy and is contributing to the achievement of business outcomes.
- **Retiring services** Decommissioning or formally removing the service from live use. It is removed from the service catalogue and cannot be requested. It is also removed from live use through service transition processes.
- **Refreshing the portfolio** The chief information officer (CIO) is responsible for the balance of investments, and relies on service portfolio management for monitoring, measuring and re-assessing these investments. A regular, formal review of the portfolio compares the services and investments with the IT strategy and the overall organizational strategy.

4.2.6   Triggers, inputs, outputs and interfaces

Triggers for service portfolio management include:

- Creation of a new strategy, or a change to an existing strategy
- Business relationship management receiving a request for a new service or a change to an existing service
- Service improvement opportunities from CSI

- Feedback from design, build and transition teams indicating the status of the service
- Service level management reviews that identify a service is not meeting expected outcomes or is not being used as intended
- Financial management for IT services indicating that a service costs significantly more or less than anticipated.

Inputs to service portfolio management include:

- Strategy plans
- Service improvement opportunities
- Financial reports
- Requests, suggestions or complaints from the business
- Project updates for services in the charter stage of the process.

Outputs from service portfolio management include:

- An up-to-date service portfolio
- Service charters
- Reports on the status of new or changed services
- Reports on the investment made in services in the service portfolio, and the returns on that investment
- Change proposals.

Major service portfolio management interfaces include:

- Service portfolio management determines which services will be placed into the service catalogue, while service catalogue management performs all the activities required for this to be done.
- Strategy management for IT services determines what type of services should be included in the portfolio.
- Financial management for IT services provides information and tools to enable service portfolio management to perform ROI calculations.

■ Demand management provides information about patterns of business activity.

■ Business relationship management initiates requests and obtains business information and requirements to define services and evaluate their return on investment. Business relationship management also keeps customers informed about the status of services.

■ All service design processes ensure that services can meet the performance and quality objectives specified in service portfolio management.

■ Service transition processes ensure that tools and procedures are in place to introduce the service and check that it is deployed appropriately.

■ Continual service improvement provides feedback about the actual use and return of services against anticipated performance. This is used to improve services and change the mix of services in the service portfolio.

4.2.7 Critical success factors and key performance indicators

Examples of CSFs and KPIs for service portfolio management include:

■ **CSF** The existence of a formal process to investigate and decide which services to provide

– **KPI** A formal service portfolio management process exists under the ownership of the service portfolio management process owner

– **KPI** The service portfolio management process is audited and reviewed annually and meets its objectives

■ **CSF** A model to analyse the potential return on investment and acceptable level of risk for new services or changes to existing services

– **KPI** Every service has a documented statement of the initial investment made in the service

– **KPI** Accounting records are produced on a monthly or quarterly basis to show the ongoing investment in each service. These are compared with the business outcomes achieved, and the return on investment is calculated.

4.2.8 Challenges and risks

Challenges for service portfolio management include:

■ Lack of access to customer business information
■ Absence of formal project management
■ Absence of a project portfolio, customer portfolio or customer agreement portfolio
■ A service portfolio focusing only on service provider aspects of services, making it difficult to calculate the value of services, model future utilization or validate customer requirements
■ Lack of a formal change management process.

Service portfolio management risks include:

■ Customer pressure resulting in a rushed decision taken before service portfolio management has completed a full investigation of risks
■ Offering services without defining how they will be measured.

4.3   FINANCIAL MANAGEMENT FOR IT SERVICES

The term 'financial management' is used in three different ways in ITIL:

■ **Financial management** The generic use of the term
■ **Enterprise financial management** The process as it is used by the 'corporate' financial department
■ **Financial management for IT services** The way in which the IT service provider has applied the process.

4.3.1   Purpose and objectives

The purpose of financial management for IT services is to secure the appropriate level of funding to design, develop and deliver services that meet the strategy of the organization. It also acts as a gatekeeper, ensuring that the service provider does not commit to services it is unable to provide. Financial management for IT services identifies the balance between the cost and quality of service and maintains the balance of supply and demand between the service provider and its customers.

Objectives of financial management for IT services include:

■ Defining and maintaining a framework to identify, manage and communicate the cost of providing services
■ Evaluating the financial impact of new or changed strategies
■ Securing funding to manage the provision of services
■ Facilitating good stewardship of service and customer assets to ensure the organization meets its objectives
■ Understanding the relationship between expenses and income and ensuring these are balanced
■ Managing and reporting expenditure on service provision
■ Executing the organization's financial policies and practices
■ Accounting for money spent on the creation, delivery and support of services
■ Forecasting financial requirements for meeting service commitments, and compliance with regulatory and legislative requirements
■ Where appropriate, defining a framework to recover the costs of service provision from the customer.

4.3.2   Scope

Financial management is normally a well-established and well-understood part of any organization. Professional accountants manage dedicated finance departments, which set financial policies, budgeting procedures, reporting standards, accounting practices and revenue generation or cost recovery rules.

In an IT context, financial management is often a separate function reporting to the CIO or the chief financial officer (CFO).

4.3.3 Value to business

Specific benefits to the business include:

- The ability to conduct business in a financially responsible manner and to comply with regulatory and legislative requirements and accepted accounting principles
- Accurate planning and forecasting of the budget to deliver services
- Better matching of IT services to business outcomes results in improved spending models and more predictable profitability
- The ability to make sound business decisions regarding the use of and investment in IT.

4.3.4 Policies, principles and basic concepts

4.3.4.1 Enterprise financial management policies

Financial management for IT services is an application of the financial management policies and practices of the organization as a whole and must therefore follow these policies and practices.

An important policy decision is whether IT will be a profit or cost centre:

- **Cost centre** A business unit or department to which costs are assigned, but which does not charge for services. It is expected to account for the money it spends, and perhaps also to show a return on the investment.
- **Profit centre** A business unit that charges for services. It does not have to make profits; it may run at a loss or break even.

4.3.4.2   Funding

Funding refers to the financial resources an IT service provider obtains to pay for the design, transition, operation and improvement of IT services. Funding comes from two sources:

- **External funding** Revenue received from selling services to external customers
- **Internal funding** This comes from other business units in the same organization.

The choice depends on whether IT is viewed as a cost or a profit centre.

4.3.4.3   Value

Appropriate financial management practices must be in place for both the service provider and its customers, since the calculation of value is a joint responsibility. If they calculate costs and returns differently, it will be impossible to demonstrate the value of IT services.

4.3.4.4   Compliance

Compliance is the ability to demonstrate that proper accounting methods and/or practices are being employed consistently. This relates to financial asset valuation, capitalization practices, revenue recognition, access and security controls etc. Enterprise financial management policies must specify the legislative and regulatory requirements that apply to the service provider and customer's organization.

4.3.5   Process activities, methods and techniques

The major inputs, outputs and activities of financial management for IT services are illustrated in Figure 4.5 and described in the rest of section 4.3.

4.3.5.1   Major inputs

Major inputs of financial management for IT services include:

- **Regulatory requirements** Prevent fraudulent activity, ensure that stakeholders' interests are protected and facilitate ethical and legal activity by the organization and its leaders
- **Enterprise financial management policies** Define how enterprise financial management works and how it relates to activities in the business units
- **Service management processes** Provide financial information
- **Service, contract, customer, application and project portfolios** Contain financial information used to analyse investments in services and corresponding returns
- **Service knowledge management system** Provides specific information about service assets and related investments.

4.3.5.2   Accounting

Accounting is the process responsible for identifying the actual costs of delivering IT services, comparing these with budgeted costs and managing variance from budget. Accounting also tracks income earned by services.

Cost model

A cost model is a framework used to record and categorize costs and allocate them to customers, business units or projects. If financial management for IT services can link costs to specific services and customers, it can predict how changes will impact the cost of IT, allowing service provider managers and customers to make better decisions about service requirements and delivery options.

Figure 4.5 Major inputs, outputs and activities of financial management for IT services

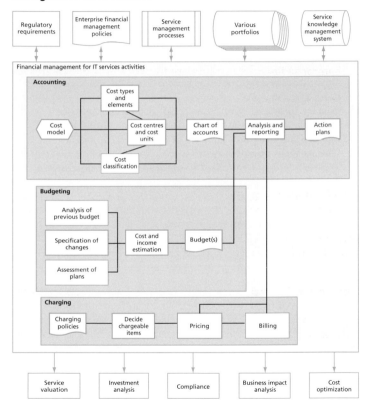

There are four main types of cost model:

- **Cost by IT organization** The IT organization accounts for its costs and reports these to financial management. Costs are analysed and allocated to business units and other functions according to the number of users, number of PCs, percentage utilization of IT services etc.
- **Cost by service** Costs of IT are allocated to a specific service. The customer determines whether the service adds value or is too expensive.
- **Cost by customer** The actual cost of tangible items used by a customer is passed to them, sometimes in combination with other allocated costs.
- **Cost by location** Similar to cost by customer, except that the costs are passed to a location, such as a regional office.

Organizations rarely use a single cost model for all services; most choose a hybrid cost model.

Cost centres and cost units

In the context of cost models and accounting systems, a cost centre is anything to which a cost can be allocated – for example, a service, location, department, business unit etc. That cost centre might become the basis for a charging policy or billing method.

A cost unit is a category within a cost centre which enables a service provider to break down the cost centre into more specific terms.

Cost types and cost elements

Cost types are categories of expense that are defined in terms of the service provider's structure. These can be broken down into cost elements (sub-categories of cost types).

Cost classification

Cost classification enables an organization to forecast the behaviour of costs over time. Most cost elements behave in a predictable way if financial management for IT services is able to link them to business activity.

There are six major classifications, grouped in pairs as follows:

- **Capital or operational** A capital cost is the cost of purchasing something that will become a financial, or fixed, asset that is subject to depreciation. An operational cost is any ongoing cost.
- **Direct or indirect** Direct costs can be allocated in full to a specific customer, service, cost centre, project, etc. Indirect costs are used by, and have to be allocated to, more than one customer, cost centre, project, etc.
- **Fixed or variable** Fixed costs do not vary with IT service usage. Variable costs depend on how much an IT service is used or on something else that cannot be fixed in advance.

Depreciation is a measure of the reduction in value of an asset over its life, and is determined by enterprise financial management policies or legislation. Depreciation allows an organization to account for the cost of an asset over several years, and to build reserves for replacing it.

Chart of accounts

The chart of accounts is a list of all the accounts recording income and expenses. It is defined and managed by enterprise financial management. In a Type III provider (see section 3.3), it is likely that the chart of accounts is set up according to the types of services delivered and their customers. In internal service providers the chart of accounts will probably be defined according to the type of business the organization conducts.

Financial management for IT services must align the chart of accounts with its own cost models, services and expenditure. Some IT departments create their own charts of accounts and align them with that of the enterprise.

Analysis and reporting

Although most financial reporting has some standard reports, these might not adequately represent IT's requirements or communicate the value of IT services. Accountants should understand what IT needs to know to deliver and manage services; IT must understand what the accountants need to know to produce that information.

Action plans

If financial analysis and reports show that the organization is on track to achieve its financial targets, little change is required. If there is significant deviation from agreed financial targets, an action plan is needed. These action plans are normally short-term, and are aimed at restoring the organization to its planned path within a month or quarter, or else getting stakeholders to change the plans and targets.

Reporting budget deviation on its own achieves little but awareness. A budget deviation with an associated action plan is a powerful management tool.

4.3.5.3   Budgeting

Budgeting is the activity of predicting and controlling the spending of money using a periodic negotiation cycle to set future budgets (usually annual) alongside routine monitoring and adjustment.

A budget is a list of all the monies an organization or business unit plans to receive, and to pay out, over a specified period of time. It takes into account existing spending, and how this will change during the next financial year. In addition the budget forecasts investments in new or changed services.

The budgeting process, policies and documents are defined and managed by enterprise financial management. IT does not 'own' the budgeting process, although it does make a commitment to achieve the performance of a budget.

Budgeting consists of the following major activities:

- **Analysis of previous budget** Analyse the previous year's budget to detect trends and to look for mistakes.
- **Assessment of plans** Several plans are taken into account when budgeting, including strategic, project, capacity, availability and service improvement plans.
- **Specification of changes to funding and spending** These include contract changes, management policies and financial policies.
- **Cost and income estimation** The categories in the budget worksheet are completed, as defined by the organization's financial office.

4.3.5.4   Charging

Charging is the activity whereby payment is required for services delivered. For internal service providers charging is optional (many organizations treat their IT service provider as a cost centre). In this situation charging is often referred to as 'chargeback' (service provider costs are re-allocated to other business units by central finance using an internal charging mechanism).

Type III service providers always charge for their services. This is not 'chargeback' since services are generally sold at a profit.

Charging policies

Charging policies determine how charging will work, and are defined by the office of the CFO or financial controller which decides:

- ■ Whether or not to charge.
- ■ The level of cost recovery that needs to be achieved. Options include break even, recovery with additional margin, cross-subsidization and notional charging.
- ■ How to use charging to manage behaviour.
- ■ How to deal with customers who decide to source IT services externally.
- ■ The level of monitoring that will be performed.

Decide chargeable items

Chargeable items are things that can be perceived and controlled by the customer, who can manage their budget by adjusting their demand for these items.

Pricing

Pricing establishes how much customers will be charged, depending on what the chargeable item is, which cost units are associated with the chargeable item, and policies about cost recovery. Pricing options include:

- ■ Cost
- ■ Cost plus
- ■ Going rate
- ■ Market price
- ■ Fixed price

- Tiered subscription
- Differential charging.

Billing

Billing is the process of producing and presenting an invoice to a customer. There are three main options:

- No billing
- Informational billing (used with notional charging)
- Billing and collection (real charging).

4.3.6 Triggers, inputs, outputs and interfaces

Triggers for financial management for IT services include:

- Monthly, quarterly and annual financial reporting cycles
- Audits
- Requests for financial information from other service management processes
- Investigation into a new service opportunity
- The introduction of charging for IT services
- A request for change.

The major inputs to financial management for IT services are illustrated in Figure 4.5 and discussed in more detail in section 4.3.5.1.

Major outputs of financial management for IT services are:

- Service valuation, i.e. understanding the costs of a service relative to its business value
- Service investment analysis
- Compliance
- Cost optimization
- Business impact analysis (BIA).

Major interfaces with financial management for IT services include:

- **Strategy management for IT services** Works with enterprise financial management to determine financial objectives for the organization.
- **Service portfolio management** Provides the service structure used to define cost models, accounting and budgeting systems and the basis for charging.
- **Business relationship management** Provides information about how the business measures the value of services and what they are prepared to pay.
- **Capacity and availability management** Provide information about options of technology and service performance.
- **Change management** Uses financial management for IT services to help determine financial impact or requirements of changes.
- **Service asset and configuration management** Documents financial data about assets and configuration items.
- **Continual service improvement** Uses financial management for IT services to determine whether the return of an improvement will be cost-effective.

4.3.7 Critical success factors and key performance indicators

Examples of CSFs and KPIs for financial management for IT services include:

- **CSF** There is an enterprise-wide framework to identify, manage and communicate financial information, and this includes the cost and associated return of services
  - **KPI** Enterprise financial management has established standards, policies and charts of accounts which it requires all business units to comply with. Audits indicate the extent of compliance
- **CSF** Financial management for IT services is a key component of evaluating strategies

– **KPI** All strategies have a comprehensive analysis of investment and returns, conducted with information from financial management for IT services.

4.3.8   Challenges and risks

Challenges for financial management for IT services include:

■ Financial reporting and cost models that are focused on the cost of infrastructure and applications rather than the cost of services.

■ Chart-of-accounts categories being meaningful to IT departments, and also mapped to enterprise financial systems.

■ If the organization focuses on cost saving rather than cost optimization, financial management for IT services will be identifying cost-cutting measures rather than demonstrating return on investment and value.

■ When financial management for IT services is first introduced or formalized, it may be difficult locate financial data and establish how it is controlled.

■ Internal service providers may find it difficult to introduce charging.

■ External service providers must balance the cost of services with their perceived value to ensure correct pricing models.

Financial management for IT services risks include:

■ Introducing financial management processes for an internal service provider may be viewed as a waste of money and time. However, lack of financial management for IT services could result in poor investment decisions which would far outweigh the costs of implementing financial management.

- Organizations that do not have adequate financial management processes for IT services may be exposed to penalties for non-compliance with legislative or regulatory requirements.
- Staff should be available who understand the world of the service provider, as well as the world of cost accounting.

4.4   DEMAND MANAGEMENT

4.4.1   Purpose and objectives

The purpose of demand management is to understand, anticipate and influence customer demand for services and to work with capacity management to ensure that the service provider has capacity to meet this demand. Demand management operates at every stage of the lifecycle to ensure that services are designed, tested and delivered to support the achievement of business outcomes at appropriate levels of activity.

The objectives of demand management are to:

- Identify and analyse patterns of business activity
- Define and analyse user profiles
- Ensure that services are designed to meet patterns of business activity
- Work with capacity management to ensure that resources are available with appropriate capacity to meet the demand, maintaining a balance between the cost of a service and the value it achieves
- Gear resources that deliver services to meet the fluctuating levels of demand for those services.

4.4.2 Scope

Demand management is active in every stage of the service lifecycle, and works closely with several other processes. Demand management focuses primarily on the business and user aspects of providing services, whereas capacity management focuses primarily on resourcing and technology.

4.4.3 Value to business

The main value of demand management is to achieve a balance between the cost of a service and the value of its business outcomes. Other service strategy processes define the linkage between business outcomes, services, resources and capabilities. Demand management clarifies how, when and to what level these elements interact, enabling executives to evaluate the investment required to achieve business outcomes at varying levels of activity.

4.4.4 Policies, principles and basic concepts

4.4.4.1 Supply and demand

The cycle of demand and supply only functions effectively if service assets have available capacity. As soon as capacity fails, the service provider can no longer supply enough of the services to satisfy customer demand.

For this reason, demand management must understand the potential demand, and its impact on the service assets, in order to manage service assets (and investments) towards optimal performance and cost.

4.4.4.2 Gearing service assets

Balance of supply and demand is achieved by gearing service assets to meet the dynamic patterns of demand. This is not just a case of responding to demand as it occurs but anticipating the demand, identifying the signals of increasing or decreasing demand and defining a mechanism to scale investment and supply.

4.4.5   Process activities, methods and techniques

4.4.5.1   Identify sources of demand forecasting

Potential sources of information that can assist demand management include:

■ Business and marketing plans and forecasts
■ Production plans (in manufacturing environments)
■ Sales forecasts
■ New product launch plans.

4.4.5.2   Patterns of business activity

Customer assets such as people, processes and applications tend to perform business activities in patterns. These patterns of business activity (PBAs) represent the dynamics of the business and generate patterns of demand for IT services. An example is processing an order, where the pattern of activity depends on level of marketing, seasonal demand etc.

Once a PBA has been identified, details should be documented.

4.4.5.3   User profiles

A user profile (UP) is a pattern of user demand for IT services. Each user profile includes one or more PBAs.

PBAs and UPs give service providers the information necessary to serve the demand with appropriately matched services, service levels and service assets. This improves value for customers and service providers by eliminating waste and poor performance.

4.4.5.4   Activity-based demand management

Business processes are the primary source of demand for services. It is important to study the customer's business to identify, analyse and classify such patterns as a basis for capacity management.

If a business plan requires the performance of a specific activity, this can be translated into demand for a service. Changes to this activity can trigger changes in service demand. After validating the activity/demand model, adjustment can be made to account for variations.

4.4.5.5   Develop differentiated offerings

When analysing the PBA, it may become apparent that varying levels of performance are required, or different combinations of utility. In these cases, it is important to work with service portfolio management to define service packages that meet the variations in PBA.

4.4.5.6   Management of operational demand

During service operation, demand management influences the demand if services or resources are being over-utilized. Typically this would occur when:

- PBAs were inaccurate, resulting in over- or under-utilization of the service.
- The business environment changed, resulting in a change to the PBA.
- The service provider's forecast for resources was inaccurate, and there was insufficient budget to increase capacity.

4.4.6 Triggers, inputs, outputs and interfaces

Triggers for demand management include:

■ A request received from a customer for a new service, or change to an existing service
■ A new service created to meet a strategic initiative
■ A service model that needs to be defined, including PBAs and/or UPs
■ Utilization rates causing potential performance issues
■ An exception to forecast patterns of business activity.

Inputs to demand management include:

■ An initiative to create a new service, or to change an existing service
■ The customer portfolio, service portfolio and customer agreement portfolio, all of which contain information about demand and supply for services
■ Assessment of charging models to ensure that under- or over-recovery does not occur in internal service providers or that pricing will be profitable for external service providers
■ Service improvement opportunities and plans.

Outputs of demand management include:

■ Formally documented patterns of business activity and user profiles
■ Policies for management of demand when resources are over-utilized
■ Policies covering situations where service utilization is higher or lower than anticipated by the customer
■ Documentation of options for differentiated offerings.

Major interfaces with demand management include:

- **Strategy management for IT services** Identifies key business outcomes and business activities to establish patterns of business activity and user profiles.
- **Service portfolio management** Uses information from demand management to create and evaluate service models, to forecast utilization and identify types of user.
- **Financial management for IT services** Helps to forecast the cost of satisfying the demand based on forecast PBAs.
- **Business relationship management** The primary source of information about business activities of the customer.
- **Service level management** Formalizes agreements in which the customer commits to levels of utilization, and the service provider commits to levels of performance.
- **Capacity management** Works with demand management to match supply and demand in the design and operation of the service.
- **Availability management** Uses information about PBAs to determine when service availability is most important.
- **IT service continuity management** Uses demand management information to help with sizing recovery options.
- **Change management** Works with demand management to assess the impact of changes on how the business uses services.
- **Service validation and testing** Ensures that the service correctly deals with patterns of demand, and that measures to prevent over-utilization are effective.
- **Event management** Can provide information about actual patterns of service utilization and validate the PBAs.

4.4.7   Critical success factors and key performance indicators

Examples of CSFs and KPIs for demand management include:

■ **CSF** The service provider has identified and analysed patterns of business activity and is able to use these to understand the levels of demand that will be placed on a service

- **KPI** Patterns of business activity are defined for each relevant service
- **KPI** Patterns of business activity have been translated into workload information by capacity management

■ **CSF** The service provider has defined and analysed user profiles and is able to use these to understand typical profiles of demand for services from different types of user

- **KPI** Documented user profiles exist and each contains a demand profile for the services used by that type of user.

4.4.8   Challenges and risks

Challenges for demand management include:

■ Availability of information about business activities
■ Customers finding it difficult to break down individual activities that make sense to the service provider
■ Lack of a formal service portfolio management process or service portfolio.

Demand management risks include:

■ Lack of, or inaccurate, configuration management information
■ Service level management being unable to obtain commitments to minimum or maximum utilization levels.

4.5   BUSINESS RELATIONSHIP MANAGEMENT

4.5.1   Purpose and objectives

The purpose of the business relationship management process is two-fold:

- Establish and maintain a business relationship between the service provider and the customer based on understanding the customer and their business needs
- Identify customer needs and ensure that the service provider is able to meet these needs as they change over time and according to circumstances.

The objectives of business relationship management include:

- Ensure that the service provider understands the customer's perspective
- Ensure high levels of customer satisfaction, and that customer requirements are met
- Establish and maintain a constructive relationship between the service provider and the customer based on understanding the customer's needs
- Identify changes to the customer environment
- Identify technology trends that could potentially impact services
- Establish and articulate business requirements for new or changed services
- Work with customers to ensure that services and service levels can deliver value
- Mediate to resolve conflicting requirements from different business units
- Establish formal complaints and escalation processes.

4.5.2   Scope

Business relationship management depends on several other service management processes and functions. Unless relationships between business relationship management and these processes are clearly identified, there is potential for confusion. Business relationship management should focus on the relationship between the service provider and its customers and levels of customer satisfaction, whereas other processes focus on the services, and the extent to which they meet the stated requirements.

For example, business relationship management and service level management both involve significant interface with customers. Staff should be aware of their different roles in building customer relationships and defining customer requirements, versus defining and coordinating the performance of specific services.

4.5.3   Value to business

The value of business relationship management lies in the ability of the service provider to articulate and meet the business needs of its customers by creating a forum for ongoing, structured communication. This enables business relationship management to achieve better alignment and integration of services in the future, as well as to fulfil current business outcomes.

This communication promotes greater understanding of the customer's business and improved customer knowledge of the service provider's capabilities and services. It helps to set realistic customer expectations, and puts a human face on the service provider.

4.5.4.1   Business relationship management and the business relationship manager

The business relationship management process is often confused with the business relationship manager role. The business relationship manager often represents other processes when engaged in business relationship management – for example, when obtaining information about customer requirements and business outcomes, they also provide this input to service portfolio management, demand management and capacity management. Thus, it may seem unclear which process the business relationship manager role is executing.

4.5.4.2   Customer portfolio

A customer portfolio is a database or structured document recording all customers of the IT service provider. It is the business relationship manager's view of these customers.

The customer portfolio is used in several processes, especially service portfolio management, but it is defined and maintained in the business relationship management process. The customer portfolio allows the service provider to quantify its commitments, investments and risks for each customer.

4.5.4.3   Customer agreement portfolio

The customer agreement portfolio is a database or structured document used to manage service contracts or agreements between an IT service provider and its customers.

This is an important tool for business relationship management, but it is usually defined and maintained as part of service level management to ensure alignment of services with agreements. It is difficult to achieve economies of scale, and to deliver shared services, if each contract is managed from a different baseline. It is therefore vital to coordinate all commitments across all agreements.

4.5.4.4 Customer satisfaction

To safeguard customer satisfaction, business relationship management works throughout the service lifecycle to understand customer requirements and expectations, and guarantee they are met or exceeded. In *service strategy*, business relationship management ensures that the service provider understands the customer's objectives and overall requirements. At all stages of the service pipeline, business relationship management represents the customer's perspective and requirements. It also makes the customer aware of the service provider's constraints and requirements.

In *service design*, business relationship management provides guidance to both the customer and the design teams about who to communicate with, and what to communicate. Business relationship management also checks that the service provider has properly understood the customer's requirements.

In *service transition*, business relationship management ensures that the customer is involved in change, release and deployment activities that impact their services, checking that their feedback has been considered. The business relationship manager may represent the customer on the change advisory board (CAB), or arrange for the customer to be at CAB and change evaluation meetings when appropriate.

In *service operation*, business relationship management works with service level management, incident management and the service desk to ensure that services are delivered according to the contract or SLA.

In *continual service improvement*, business relationship management monitors service reports and receives frequent updates about customer satisfaction, exceptions to service levels and customer requests or complaints.

Business relationship management measures customer satisfaction and compares service provider performance with customer satisfaction targets and previous scores, commonly assessed by a regular survey.

Business relationship management also defines how to differentiate between customer and user satisfaction, and ensures that both are measured appropriately.

4.5.4.5   Service requirements

Throughout the service lifecycle, business relationship management helps to define and clarify requirements for services. This involves investigating the business need, validating it, defining a business case and evaluating the warranty and utility needed.

4.5.4.6   Business relationship management as facilitator of strategic partnerships

Some service providers are so important to their customer that they are included in strategic discussions about the customer's business, even forming part of the CEO or CIO steering group. Business relationship management facilitates this, and ensures that appropriate people attend these meetings.

4.5.5   Process activities, methods and techniques

4.5.5.1   Initiation by customers

Customers need a way to communicate with the service provider about their needs and opportunities.

Business relationship management provides a point of coordination for all customer requirements, so that customers can deal with the appropriate staff at a suitable time without having to worry whether their requests will be met. The only exceptions are routine interfaces between service provider and customer staff during the delivery of services; and the coordination provided by the service desk in resolving incidents or standard service requests.

Business relationship management provides a customer interface for:

- A potential business opportunity
- A request for change
- Other requests, such as help in evaluating whether a new technology represents a business opportunity
- Complaints and compliments.

4.5.5.2   Initiation by the service provider

The service provider initiates the business relationship management process if they need input from customers, or if they need to start a new service or change an existing service.

The business relationship manager is usually responsible for executing business relationship management – although some aspects could be automated or delegated. The business relationship manager must maintain a register of all opportunities, requests, complaints and compliments to track them and ensure that they are not overlooked.

4.5.5.3   The business relationship management process through the service lifecycle

- **Service strategy** Business relationship management applies strategies, policies and plans to coordinate the service provider's processes with customer requirements and opportunities. Strategy management for IT services identifies key market spaces and business opportunities. Business relationship management ensures that these are appropriately defined and executed from a customer perspective.

■ **Service design** Business relationship management ensures that the design and development of services continue to meet customer requirements, and that they support the identified business outcomes. Business relationship management focuses on the functionality (utility) of the services, but it also assures customers of warranty.

■ **Service transition** Business relationship management coordinates customer involvement in service transition, ensuring that changes and releases meet customer requirements.

■ **Service operation** Business relationship management detects changes in how services are used. Although the service desk can deal with most incidents and requests, some require a higher level of involvement and communication.

■ **Continual service improvement** Business relationship management helps to identify improvement opportunities and coordinates both service provider and customer activities to achieve this improvement. It conducts customer satisfaction surveys, identifying areas for improvement and new opportunities.

4.5.6 Triggers, inputs, outputs and interfaces

Triggers for business relationship management include:

■ Launch of a new strategic initiative
■ A new service, or a change to an existing service
■ Identification of a new opportunity
■ A service chartered by service portfolio management
■ Customer requests, suggestions or complaints
■ A customer meeting
■ A customer satisfaction survey.

Inputs to business relationship management include:

- Customer requirements, requests, complaints, escalations or compliments
- The service strategy
- Where possible, the customer's strategy
- The service portfolio
- The project portfolio
- Service level agreements
- Requests for change
- Patterns of business activity and user profiles.

Outputs of business relationship management include:

- Stakeholder definitions
- Defined business outcomes
- Agreement to fund (internal) or pay for (external) services
- The customer portfolio
- Service requirements for strategy, design and transition
- Customer satisfaction surveys, and the published results of these surveys
- Schedules of customer activity in service management process activities
- Schedule of training and awareness events
- Reports on customer perception of service performance.

Major interfaces with business relationship management include:

- **Strategy management for IT services** works with business relationship management to identify market spaces. Business relationship management is also instrumental in gathering strategic requirements, identifying desired business outcomes and securing funding (internal) or pursuing deals (external).

- **Service portfolio management** and business relationship management work together to identify requirements and information about the customer environment.
- Business relationship management helps **financial management for IT services** to obtain information about the customer's financial objectives and assists the service provider in understanding which levels of funding or pricing the customer will accept.
- Business relationship management assists **demand management** to identify and validate patterns of business activity and user profiles.
- **Service level management** uses information about customers and service requirements gathered during the business relationship management process to understand customer priorities.
- **Capacity management** and **availability management** rely on information about business outcomes and service requirements gathered through business relationship management.
- Business relationship management helps ensure that **service continuity plans** and tests accurately represent the world of the customer – and thus increase the level of assurance.
- Business relationship management often initiates **requests for change** and also helps to assess changes.
- Business relationship management ensures appropriate customer involvement in **release and deployment management**, and **service validation and testing**.
- Service improvements and **the seven-step improvement process** are important features of business relationship management.

Examples of CSFs and KPIs for business relationship management include:

- **CSF** The ability to document and understand customer requirements of services, and the business outcomes they wish to achieve
  - **KPI** Business outcomes and customer requirements are documented and signed off by the customer as input into service portfolio management and service design processes
- **CSF** The ability to measure customer satisfaction levels, and to know what action to take with the results
  - **KPI** Customer satisfaction levels are consistently high and feed back into service portfolio management and strategy management for IT services. Any score lower than a defined level triggers an investigation into the cause and corrective action – involving service level management, problem management, capacity management etc.

Challenges for business relationship management include:

- If business relationship management is simply a means of managing customer satisfaction, it will probably fail. Business relationship management should be involved in defining services, and tracking that they are delivered to agreed levels.
- A history of poor service may make it difficult for business relationship management to function effectively.
- Lack of clarity between the role of business relationship manager and the process of business relationship management can cause confusion.

Business relationship management risks include:

- Business relationship management is closely related to other processes. Confusion about the boundaries between these processes will create the potential for duplication of activity, interference or neglect of activities.
- A disconnect between customer-facing processes, such as business relationship management, and those focusing more on technology, such as capacity management, is likely to make the service provider ineffective.

5 Organizing for service strategy

There is no single best way to organize, and best practices described in ITIL need to be tailored to suit each situation, taking into account resource constraints and the size, nature and needs of the business and customers. The starting point for organizational design is service strategy.

Section 2.2.3 of this publication provides an overview of functions and roles.

5.1 FUNCTIONS

For service strategy to be successful, an organization will need to define the roles and responsibilities required to undertake the processes and activities identified in this key element guide. These roles should be assigned to individuals, and an appropriate organization structure of teams, groups or functions established and managed.

Service strategy does not define specific functions, but it does rely on the technical and application management functions described in *ITIL Service Operation*. Technical and application management provide resources and expertise to manage the whole service lifecycle, and roles within service strategy may be performed by members of these functions.

5.2 ROLES

A number of roles need to be performed in support of service strategy. The core ITIL publications provide guidelines and examples of role descriptions. In many cases roles will need to be combined or separated depending on the organizational context and size.

A RACI model can be used to define the roles and responsibilities in relation to processes and activities.

RACI is an acronym for:

- **Responsible** The person or people responsible for correct execution – for getting the job done.
- **Accountable** The person who has ownership of quality and the end result.
- **Consulted** The people who are consulted and whose opinions are sought. They have involvement through input of knowledge and information.
- **Informed** The people who are kept up to date on progress. They receive information about process execution and quality.

Only one person should be accountable for any process or individual activity, although several people may be responsible for executing parts of the activity.

Roles fall into two main categories – generic roles such as process manager and process owner, and specific roles that are involved within a particular lifecycle stage or process, such as a change administrator or knowledge management process owner.

5.2.1 Generic service owner role

The service owner is accountable for the delivery of a specific IT service and is responsible for the initiation, transition, maintenance and support of that service.

The service owner's responsibilities include:

- Working with business relationship management to ensure that the service provider can meet customer requirements
- Participating in negotiating service level agreements (SLAs) and operational level agreements (OLAs) relating to the service

- Ensuring that ongoing service delivery and support meet agreed customer requirements
- Ensuring consistent and appropriate communication with customer(s) for service-related enquiries and issues
- Representing the service across the organization, including at change advisory board (CAB) meetings
- Serving as the point of escalation (notification) for major incidents relating to the service
- Participating in internal and external service review meetings.

The service owner is responsible for continual improvement and the management of change affecting the service under their care.

5.2.2 Generic process owner role

The process owner role is accountable for ensuring that a process is fit for purpose, is performed according to agreed standards and meets the aims of the process definition. This role is often assigned to the same person who carries out the process manager role, but the two roles may be separate in larger organizations.

The process owner's accountabilities include:

- Sponsoring, designing and change managing the process and its metrics
- Defining appropriate policies and standards for the process, with periodic auditing to ensure compliance
- Providing process resources to support activities required throughout the service lifecycle
- Ensuring that process technicians understand their role and have the required knowledge to deliver the process
- Addressing issues with running the process
- Identifying enhancement and improvement opportunities and making improvements to the process.

5.2.3 Generic process manager role

The process manager role is accountable for operational management of a process. There may be several process managers for one process, for example covering different locations.

The process manager's accountabilities include:

- Working with the process owner to plan and coordinate all process activities
- Ensuring that all activities are carried out as required throughout the service lifecycle
- Appointing people to the required roles and managing assigned resources
- Monitoring and reporting on process performance
- Identifying opportunities for and making improvements to the process.

5.2.4 Generic process practitioner role

The process practitioner's responsibilities include:

- Carrying out one or more activities of a process
- Understanding how their role contributes to the overall delivery of service and creation of value for the business
- Ensuring that inputs, outputs and interfaces for their activities are correct
- Creating or updating records to show that activities have been carried out correctly.

5.2.5 Strategy management for IT services roles

5.2.5.1 Strategy management for IT services process owner

Responsibilities typically include:

- Carrying out the generic process owner role for strategy management for IT services

■ Working with other process owners to ensure that the organization's overall IT strategy is effectively reflected in their processes.

5.2.5.2 Strategy management for IT services process manager

Responsibilities typically include:

■ Carrying out the generic process manager role for strategy management for IT services
■ Strategic assessment
■ Strategy generation
■ Strategy execution
■ Measurement and evaluation (through continual service improvement).

5.2.5.3 Business strategy manager

The business strategy manager is responsible for working with all business units (including IT) to ensure that all strategic planning and execution are linked as part of the enterprise strategy.

5.2.5.4 IT steering group

The IT steering group will be made up of company owners, board directors, chief officers, senior managers or others appointed on their behalf. In most organizations this will also include one or more enterprise architects. The steering group is responsible for corporate governance of IT.

The group will steer the overall direction of the IT strategy, its implementation and the ongoing activities within the IT organization, to underpin the organization's business strategy and meet the desired business outcomes. The IT steering group is also responsible for financial planning and scheduling of execution activities.

5.2.5.5 IT director or service management director

Medium and larger organizations may appoint an IT director or service management director to be responsible for all ITSM processes and/or to establish a service management office. These role titles vary based on the culture of the organization (e.g. vice president or manager may be more appropriate than director).

This role is responsible for the overall implementation and operation of IT service management throughout the service lifecycle.

5.2.6 Service portfolio management roles

5.2.6.1 Service portfolio management process owner

Responsibilities typically include:

- Carrying out the generic process owner role for service portfolio management
- Working with other process owners to ensure an integrated approach to the design and implementation of service portfolio management.

5.2.6.2 Service portfolio management process manager

Responsibilities typically include:

- Carrying out the generic process manager role for service portfolio management
- Defining services and service packages and changes to these
- Defining the service portfolio and service models
- Reviewing the service portfolio
- Analysing required investments and articulating a business case for new services or changes to existing services
- Working through change management to propose changes, and to charter the activity to design and transition services

■ Monitoring design and transition activity and updating the service portfolio and stakeholders.

5.2.7 Financial management for IT services roles

Many organizations will have a person with the job title 'IT financial manager'. This job typically combines the roles of financial management for IT services process owner and financial management for IT services process manager.

5.2.7.1 Financial management for IT services process owner

Responsibilities typically include:

■ Carrying out the generic process owner role for financial management for IT services
■ Working with other process owners to ensure an integrated approach to the design and implementation of financial management for IT services.

5.2.7.2 Financial management for IT services process manager

Responsibilities typically include:

■ Carrying out the generic process manager role for financial management for IT services
■ Defining, maintaining and reporting the financial models and information required to track the cost and value of IT services
■ Budgeting for IT expenditure
■ Relating the cost of IT to the services it provides
■ In organizations where charging has been instituted, the role also formulates and manages charging systems for IT services.

5.2.7.3 Budget holders

Various IT managers may be nominated as budget holders to estimate, agree and manage budgets for their own particular area(s).

5.2.8.1   Demand management process owner

Responsibilities typically include:

- Carrying out the generic process owner activities for demand management
- Working with other process owners to ensure an integrated approach to the design and implementation of demand management.

5.2.8.2   Demand management process manager

Responsibilities typically include:

- Carrying out the generic process manager role for demand management
- Identifying and documenting patterns of business activity
- Identifying and documenting user profiles
- Working with other processes to ensure that IT capabilities are geared to meet the fluctuating demands of the business.

5.2.9.1   Business relationship manager

Many organizations have a person with the job title 'business relationship manager'. This may combine the roles of business relationship management process owner and business relationship management process manager.

'Business relationship manager' may also represent a number of individuals working within business relationship management and focused on different customer segments or groups. In some organizations, this role may be combined with the role of service level manager.

5.2.9.2   Business relationship management process owner

Responsibilities typically include:

- Carrying out the generic process owner role for business relationship management
- Working with other process owners to ensure an integrated approach to the design and implementation of business relationship management.

5.2.9.3   Business relationship management process manager

Responsibilities typically include:

- Carrying out the generic process manager role for business relationship management
- Working with customers to define needs, set expectations and measure levels of customer satisfaction
- Assessing the customer environment and the potential impact of technology trends
- Handling customer complaints and compliments
- Processing customer requests.

The business relationship management process manager actively works to establish and maintain a constructive working relationship between the service provider and the customers and users of the services provided.

5.2.9.4   Customers/users

The customers and users of the IT services are the other side of business relationship management, and engage with business relationship management to voice their needs and participate in the relationship to help ensure that business outcomes are supported.

5.2.10 Sourcing roles

Sourcing roles are defined more or less formally in different organizations. In the most formal, a sourcing office may be established and the role of chief sourcing officer defined. Whether this is represented as a full-time function or not, the key aspects of the role should be formalized and assigned to an individual or team.

The chief sourcing officer ensures that a sourcing strategy is defined and executed, and that the necessary resources and capabilities are available to meet the service demands of the organization.

6 Implementing service strategy

6.1 IMPLEMENTATION THROUGH THE LIFECYCLE

Strategies are executed in the same way as for any other initiative, through each stage of the lifecycle. In this way resources and capabilities are developed and deployed to enable the organization to reach its strategic objectives.

6.2 SERVICE STRATEGY IMPLEMENTATION ACTIVITIES FOLLOWING A LIFECYCLE APPROACH

The service provider's strategy must be continually adjusted and refined to meet changing customer requirements and strategies. Implementing service strategy is not just a case of designing and deploying static processes and ensuring that the same actions are performed consistently year after year. As services move through the service lifecycle, so too must the implementation and improvement of the service strategy processes.

6.2.1 Setting the implementation strategy

The strategy for the implementation should include:

- Current state assessment
- Target state definition
- Gap analysis
- Project identification
- Project estimation
- Project consolidation
- Roadmap.

Additional areas to take into account include:

- Even if there is no formal service strategy, the culture of the organization and its decision-making process are a de facto strategy. The initiative should take this into account.
- Implementation should include feedback mechanisms so that decision makers can adjust plans according to environmental changes.
- Executive ownership is critical for success.

6.2.2   Designing service strategy

In this stage of the lifecycle the processes, tools and organizational structure are designed. Design includes collection of detailed requirements for the areas to be implemented as well as actual design of the tools and procedures to be used.

New roles and organizational changes should also be designed, together with a transition and communication plan.

6.2.3   Transitioning service strategy

This stage includes process and tool development and/or procurement, together with the relevant configuration, testing, deployment and training. The processes and tools follow the same steps as any service that is transitioned, possibly including a pilot deployment, and certainly a post-implementation review.

6.2.4   Operating service strategy

This stage involves the execution of the processes described in the core *ITIL Service Strategy* publication. It also includes the maintenance of tools and processes, as well as resolving any exceptions in their operation.

6.2.5   Continual improvement of service strategy

Continual service improvement evaluates the performance of each process and the ability of the service provider to deliver valuable services. Continual service improvement also identifies and assesses opportunities to improve performance and exploit changes to the internal or external environments.

6.3   THE IMPACT OF SERVICE STRATEGY ON OTHER LIFECYCLE STAGES

Service strategy provides the direction, policies and standards whereby each stage is executed, and in which services move through the lifecycle.

6.3.1   Service strategy and service design

Service strategy sets the broad direction for the design of services. It also defines specific outcomes and objectives that services need to achieve. Service strategy therefore provides the trigger for services that must be designed, and ultimately determines whether the service provider was successful. Service strategy defines what is needed to ensure the competitiveness of the service provider and the satisfaction of its customers. Service design defines, in detail, how the service provider will achieve that.

Specific tools and procedures that have greatest impact on service design are:

■ **Defining outcomes and constraints** Determining which attributes of a service are essential, which add value and which are purely 'nice to have' is an important part of designing a service. In addition, service strategy identifies constraints under which the service should be developed.

- **Service models** Provide the basic architecture, aid in communicating the intent of the strategy and help designers understand how services will be used.
- **Patterns of business activity** Assist in the design related to utilization, performance, capacity and availability of services.
- **Business impact analysis** Although detailed BIA is defined for key services in IT service continuity management, a strategic assessment of the impact of potential service outages helps to prioritize design activity.
- **Business relationship management** This is an important source of information about the customer, and their objectives, environment and requirements. It continues to validate and clarify customer requirements throughout the service design stage.

6.3.2 Service strategy and service transition

Service transition is often seen as a tactical stage in which services are moved from design and build into operation. In fact, service transition is critical if the organization is to change its strategy. It is through service transition that the cultural, organizational and service changes occur, allowing the organization to meet its changing objectives.

Service strategy has a key impact on service transition from three points of view.

Firstly, service strategy assists in defining the strategy for transition of services.

Secondly, service strategy defines what needs to change, when and to what extent. If changes were not managed within the context of service strategy, it would be easy for numerous small changes to result in a major strategic change. Through service portfolio management and strategy management, service transition is able to ensure that all changes contribute to the achievement of the service provider's strategy.

Thirdly, service transition tests and validates that the services being introduced and changed are able to achieve the objectives and outcomes that have been defined during service strategy and service design.

6.3.3   Service strategy and service operation

Service operation is where the value that was anticipated and designed is realized. It is critical that operational activities are designed, implemented, operated and measured based on the strategic objectives and outcomes. Although operational activities are not strategic, they enable the organization to achieve its strategy. It should be possible to define the linkage between strategic outcomes and operational activities.

6.3.4   Service strategy and continual service improvement

Continual service improvement takes its lead from service strategy, using the defined strategies and desired outcomes as a basis for evaluating whether services are successful.

Continual service improvement also acts as an initiator of strategy. It assists in determining where a strategy should be changed and how it can be made more effective. It detects changes in the use and outcomes of services, and determines their ongoing relevance.

7 Challenges, risks and critical success factors

7.1 CHALLENGES

- **Complexity** The complexity of many organizations causes them to be self-stabilizing and resistant to change. Dividing a service or process into components to manage them can be useful, but it also needs greater coordination.
- **Coordination and control** Specialization allows for development of in-depth knowledge, skills and experience, and facilitates innovation, improvements and changes. However, increased specialization demands greater coordination. This is a major challenge because of the level of specialization needed for various stages of the service lifecycle, processes and functions.
- **Preserving value** New services quickly lose their attraction and become part of everyday life. It is important to maintain the customer's perception of the value of services.
- **Effective measurement** Performance measurements in service organizations are frequently out of step with the business because traditional measurements focus on internal goals rather than customer satisfaction.

7.2 RISKS

- **Inaccurate information** It is important to build good relationships and communication channels with all business units, customers and suppliers, and use these to gain timely, accurate business information.

- **Taking, or failing to take, opportunities** The opportunity costs of under-served market spaces and unfulfilled demand can be identified and managed by mapping the service portfolio to an underlying portfolio of risks. Potential benefits must be worth more than the cost to address the risk.
- **Design risks** A major cause of poor service performance is poor design. The utility of a service might also diminish with changes in the pattern of demand. Service design processes and methods can reduce such performance and demand risks.
- **Operational risks** Service operation converts operational risks into opportunities to create value for customers. This removal of risks from the customer's business is the core value proposition of many services.
- **Procedures in service transition must ensure that this filtering capability is achieved** Schedule pressures might push early delivery of new capability without the agreed warranty, leading to tensions when the service falls below the agreed quality.
- **Market risks** Effective service management helps to reduce levels of competitive risks faced by service providers by increasing the scale and scope of demand for a service catalogue.

7.3   CRITICAL SUCCESS FACTORS

To a large extent all of the challenges and risks already mentioned can be inverted to become critical success factors. There are a number of additional factors critical to the success of a service management organization:

- Experienced, skilled and trained staff with appropriate strategic vision and decision-making skills

- Adequate support and funding from the business, which must recognize the potential value IT service management can offer
- Appropriate tools for implementing processes quickly and successfully in a cost-effective way.

8 Key messages and lessons

IT service management is not just about managing operational IT processes. It is about ensuring that IT contributes to the value of an organization. Service strategy can enable this as follows:

■ Service management answers the question 'How do we manage IT?' It is not just for the data centre, or the service management team, but for every IT person regardless of their role, starting with the executives. This responsibility cannot be delegated, and service strategy shows how to do this.

■ Service strategy is all about the customer, whether internal or external. Start by understanding the business strategy, objectives and outcomes of each business unit. This requires a business relationship manager role, and a mandate from senior IT and business management. Define IT activity in terms of business outcomes, rather than activities of IT.

■ Specifically, service strategy is about making customers successful. Internal customers will improve their competitiveness; external customers will choose a service provider who can support their working methods and objectives. An IT service provider does not succeed just because they have good processes, but because they use those processes to do the things their customers need.

■ Being a service provider is a joint responsibility. IT can cause an organization to succeed or fail, so IT needs to be part of the decision-making process. Investment decisions have to be made jointly, with IT providing a range of cost and performance options, and customers justifying their choice based on demonstrable returns. Decisions on which IT services to deliver and how to deliver them are, first and foremost, business decisions.

- Service strategy seeks to match business needs with IT ability. Every tool and process in this key element guide reflects a different aspect of that equation. This should be the primary factor on the mind of practitioners who define, implement and execute service strategy processes and tools. It is impossible to implement these as IT processes divorced from the business.
- Furthermore, business needs drive the development of IT ability. While it is true that IT innovation creates business opportunities, it is the opportunity that is central, not the technology innovation itself.

9 Related guidance

This chapter provides some information about other frameworks, best practices, models and quality systems that have synergy with the ITIL service lifecycle.

9.1 RISK ASSESSMENT AND MANAGEMENT

Risk may be defined as uncertainty of outcome, whether a positive opportunity or negative threat. Formal risk management enables better decision-making based on a sound understanding of risks and their likely impact.

A number of different methodologies, standards and frameworks have been developed for risk management. Each organization should determine the approach to risk management that is best suited to its needs and circumstances.

Approaches to risk management that should be considered include:

- Office of Government Commerce (2010). *Management of Risk: Guidance for Practitioners*. TSO, London.
- ISO 31000
- ISO/IEC 27001
- Risk IT[2]

9.2 ITIL GUIDANCE AND WEB SERVICES

ITIL is part of the Best Management Practice portfolio of best-practice guidance.

---

[2] With the publication of COBIT 5, Risk IT will be included within COBIT.

The Best Management Practice website (www.best-management-practice.com) includes news, reviews, case studies and white papers on ITIL and all other Best Management Practice guidance.

The ITIL official website (www.itil-officialsite.com) contains reliable, up-to-date information on ITIL – including information on accreditation and the ITIL software scheme for the endorsement of ITIL-based tools.

Details of the core ITIL publications are:

- Cabinet Office (2011). *ITIL Service Strategy*. TSO, London.
- Cabinet Office (2011). *ITIL Service Design*. TSO, London.
- Cabinet Office (2011). *ITIL Service Transition*. TSO, London.
- Cabinet Office (2011). *ITIL Service Operation*. TSO, London.
- Cabinet Office (2011). *ITIL Continual Service Improvement*. TSO, London.

The full ITIL glossary, in English and other languages, can be accessed through the ITIL official site at:

www.itil-officialsite.com/InternationalActivities/TranslatedGlossaries.aspx

The full range of ITIL-derived and complementary publications can be found in the publications library of the Best Management Practice website at:

www.best-management-practice.com/Publications-Library/IT-Service-Management-ITIL/

9.3   QUALITY MANAGEMENT SYSTEM

Quality management focuses on product/service quality as well as the quality assurance and control of processes. Total Quality Management (TQM) is a methodology for managing continual improvement by using a quality management system.

ISO 9000:2005 describes the fundamentals of quality management systems that are applicable to all organizations which need to demonstrate their ability to consistently provide products that meet requirements. ISO 9001:2008 specifies generic requirements for a quality management system.

9.4   GOVERNANCE OF IT

ISO 9004 (Managing for the sustained success of an organization – a quality management approach) provides guidance on governance for the board and top management of an organization.

ISO/IEC 38500 is the standard for corporate governance of IT. The purpose of this standard is to promote effective, efficient and acceptable use of IT in all organizations.

9.5   COBIT

The Control OBjectives for Information and related Technology (COBIT) is a governance and control framework for IT management created by ISACA and the IT Governance Institute (ITGI).

COBIT is positioned at a high level, is driven by business requirements, covers the full range of IT activities, and concentrates on *what* should be achieved rather than *how* to achieve effective governance, management and control. ITIL provides an organization with best-practice guidance on *how* to manage and improve its processes to deliver high-quality, cost-effective IT services.

Further information about COBIT is available at www.isaca.org and www.itgi.org

9.6   ISO/IEC 20000 SERVICE MANAGEMENT SERIES

ISO/IEC 20000 is an internationally recognized standard for ITSM covering service providers who manage and deliver IT-enabled services to internal or external customers. ISO/IEC 20000-1 is aligned with other ISO management systems standards such as ISO 9001 and ISO/IEC 27001.

One of the most common routes for an organization to achieve the requirements of ISO/IEC 20000 is by adopting ITIL best practices.

Further details can be found at www.iso.org or www.isoiec20000certification.com

9.7   ENVIRONMENTAL MANAGEMENT AND GREEN/ SUSTAINABLE IT

'Green IT' refers to environmentally sustainable computing where the use and disposal of computers and printers are carried out in sustainable ways that do not have a negative impact on the environment.

The ISO 14001 series of standards for an environment management system is designed to assure internal and external stakeholders that the organization is an environmentally responsible organization.

Further details are available at www.iso.org

9.8   PROGRAMME AND PROJECT MANAGEMENT

The principles of programme management are key to delivering on time and within budget. Best management practice in this area is found in *Managing Successful Programmes* (MSP) (TSO, 2011).

Visit www.msp-officialsite.com for more information on MSP.

Portfolio, Programme and Project Offices (P3O) (TSO, 2008) is aimed at helping organizations to establish and maintain appropriate business support structures with proven roles and responsibilities.

Visit www.p3o-officialsite.com for more information on P3O.

Structured project management methods, such as PRINCE2 (PRojects IN Controlled Environments) (TSO, 2009) or the Project Management Body of Knowledge (PMBOK) developed by the Project Management Institute (PMI), can be used when improving IT services.

Visit www.prince-officialsite.com for more information on PRINCE2.

Visit www.pmi.org for more information on PMI and PMBOK.

9.9   SKILLS FRAMEWORK FOR THE INFORMATION AGE

The Skills Framework for the Information Age (SFIA) supports skills audit, planning future skill requirements, development programmes, standardization of job titles and functions, and resource allocation.

Visit www.sfia.org.uk for further details.

9.10   CARNEGIE MELLON: CMMI AND ESCM FRAMEWORK

The Capability Maturity Model Integration (CMMI) is a process improvement approach developed by the Software Engineering Institute (SEI) of Carnegie Mellon University. CMMI can be used to guide process improvement across a project, a division or an entire organization.

The eSourcing Capability Model for Service Providers (eSCM-SP) is a framework developed by ITSqc at Carnegie Mellon to improve the relationship between IT service providers and their customers.

For more information, see www.sei.cmu.edu/cmmi/

9.11   BALANCED SCORECARD

The balanced scorecard approach provides guidance for what companies should measure to provide a balanced view. The balanced scorecard suggests that the organization be viewed from four perspectives, and it is valuable to develop metrics, collect data and analyse the organization relative to each of these perspectives:

- The learning and growth perspective
- The business process perspective
- The customer perspective
- The financial perspective.

Further details are available through the balanced scorecard user community at www.scorecardsupport.com

9.12   SIX SIGMA

Six Sigma is a data-driven process improvement approach that supports continual improvement. The objective is to implement a measurement-oriented strategy focused on process improvement and defects reduction. A Six Sigma defect is defined as anything outside customer specifications.

There are two primary sub-methodologies within Six Sigma: DMAIC (Define, Measure, Analyse, Improve, Control) and DMADV (Define, Measure, Analyse, Design, Verify). DMAIC is an improvement method for existing processes for which performance does not meet expectations, or for which incremental improvements are desired. DMADV focuses on the creation of new processes.